DIRT MATTERS

The Foundation For a Healthy, Vibrant, And Effective Congregation

JIM POWELL

Foreword by Larry Osborne

WestBow
PRESS
A DIVISION OF THOMAS NELSON

WestBow Press books may be ordered through booksellers or by contacting:

WestBow Press
A Division of Thomas Nelson
1663 Liberty Drive
Bloomington, IN 47403
www.westbowpress.com
1-(866) 928-1240

ISBN: 978-1-4908-0181-0 (sc)
ISBN: 978-1-4908-0182-7 (hc)
ISBN: 978-1-4908-0180-3 (e)

Library of Congress Control Number: 2013912770

Printed in the United States of America.

WestBow Press rev. date: 7/29/2013

To my grandparents,
Junius and Rose Ufkes

CONTENTS

FOREWORD

It's no secret that lots of churches struggle.

While some ministries explode with dynamic growth and stories of changed lives, many more (actually the majority) find themselves plateaued or in decline. Many are like a swimmer treading water. They're incredibly active, but at the end of the day, they haven't gone anywhere; they're perpetually stuck in the same place. Others remind me of the little Dutch boy with his finger in the dike. Their primary goal is survival. They just want to stay open one more week.

Frankly, we shouldn't be surprised. It's no easy thing to carry out the work of God in a culture that continues to grow increasingly deaf and even defiant to the things of God. Add to that the human failings found in those of us who call ourselves Christians, and you can see why the task of carrying out and fulfilling Jesus's Great Commission can be rather daunting—and at times appear to be hopelessly out of reach.

But it doesn't have to stay that way. Churches can turn around, even those with a long history of treading water or fighting to simply keep their doors open.

But the key to turning around a struggling church and reigniting vision and passion for Jesus's Great Commission isn't found in the places that most pastors and church leaders look. It's not found in better programs, fancy marketing, or even great preaching. It's found in something far more basic. It's found at the core—this thing called culture.

Every church has one. It's made up of the values, patterns, past decisions, and current policies (both written and unwritten) that guide the day-to-day decisions that shape a church and create its destiny.

Jim Powell uses the metaphor of farming to illustrate the importance of culture. In farming, dirt matters. Without good soil, it doesn't matter what you plant or how often you water; the crop won't grow well.

It's the same in a church. Without a healthy culture, it doesn't matter what ministry methods we use; the crop won't grow well.

Jim knows what he's talking about. His ideas and insights aren't mere theory. He's put them into practice and has the fruit to prove they work. Called to pastor a church with 65 members and a long history of treading water and slow decline, he focused on changing the culture rather than merely changing the programs.

Today, that church has grown from 65 to over 1,500. And I know its health and culture firsthand. My son and daughter-in-law attended and served in the ministry while they lived in the region. I've had the privilege of visiting the church, teaching the staff, and interacting with leaders and members. That is why I applaud Jim's insights and commend them to you.

When it comes to ministry in the local church, there are no magic bullets. But there are core principles that produce greater health when followed and sabotage health when ignored. By focusing on the dirt, you can improve the harvest. And the following pages will show you exactly how to do that.

Larry Osborne
Author and pastor, North Coast Church, Vista, CA
2013

INTRODUCTION

Early in my ministry career, a small rural church asked me to supply preach. In addition to giving the sermon, they asked me to teach the Senior High Sunday School class. The only problem was that no high school students showed up. My wife and I sat in an empty room until an elderly church leader stopped by to apologize. We ended up having a conversation about the early days of the church when the congregation was thriving. He told us that many wonderful people still attended the church, even though the attendance was dwindling, and he spoke of the numerous unreached people in the area and how the congregation was struggling to connect with them. When he left, I vividly recall turning to my wife and saying, "This church has so much potential."

Several years later I was in conversations with the church I now pastor, which had been without a minister for over a year. There were no children in the nursery, a handful of teens in the youth ministry, and a fear among the leadership that, if things didn't turn around, they might need to shut the doors. I decided to call the interim minister and ask him about the church. One of the first things he said was, "This church has so much potential."

Not only have I lived with the struggle to actualize a church's potential, but I also see it when talking with other pastors and church leaders. Each year, I have the privilege of coaching and consulting with dozens of churches. Regardless of size, denomination, or location, the refrain is the same—the church has unrealized potential and should be having more of an impact.

While the details of your church story may be different, I imagine it is also similar—a collection of good people wanting to honor the Lord and make a difference in His name, but a gnawing sense that you could be doing so much more than you are. You've tried conferences, books, ministry kits; you've prayed, networked, and maybe even wept. You've had some great events and big Sundays, but still it seems that your church has not come close to making the difference you think it can.

I am absolutely convinced that one of the main reasons so many churches are struggling and feel as though they are not reaching their full impact is because they are unaware of one of the basic elements of a healthy, vibrant, and effective congregation—the soil!

That's why I'm writing this book.

In the following pages, I'll be using the biblical and practical analogy of soil to show that addressing your church's culture is absolutely essential, and I will give you some insights about cultivating it so that your congregation can fulfill God's intent. The first section explains the connection between soil and church culture and how this has a direct correlation with the health and outcomes of a congregation. The second section will illustrate this principle by sharing five specific values I call *Activators*, which show how healthy values positively affect church culture. The final section will lay out a flexible process for developing a healthier culture in an existing congregation.

But, before we go any further, I need to make a few qualifying statements that are essential for you to understand the goals and purposes of this book. Without understanding these affirmations, you may be tempted to label this as just another church growth book.

1) *Jesus wants His church to manifest fruit.* Not only did Jesus boldly state that He has appointed us to bear fruit (John 15:16), but He also showed the urgency and importance of fruit-bearing in parables (Luke 13:6-9). In addition, He told us that every tree that doesn't bear fruit will be cut down and thrown into the fire (Matthew 7:19), and He illustrated the consequences of not bearing fruit when He approached a leafy fig tree that bore no fruit. He cursed it, and it withered and died (Mark 11:12-21). Leaves without fruit do not accomplish God's vision for His church.

Sometimes I come across leaders who are content to go through the motions and look for ways to justify the lack of visible fruit in their ministry. They become defensive when confronted with the idea that perhaps God wants them to move beyond safe, easy, and predicable patterns of ministry. They show little desire to look beyond themselves in order to make a difference in their neighborhoods, communities, or world.

If you are the leader of a struggling church, I want to encourage you without laying on guilt. Yet, at the same time, this book will unapologetically challenge you to do what you can in order to allow God to bear fruit through your congregation.

2) *Fruit-bearing is grounded in faithfulness and obedience.* With the explosion of megachurches and the emphasis on church growth and leadership literature, I fear that we have sent the message that fruit-bearing is primarily revealed in attendance numbers. Big and growing churches equal successful ministry. Small or struggling churches therefore feel as though they are failing. This attitude leads to false expectations, overwhelming pressure, and a "we/they" mentality.

In the parable of the talents, Jesus said that some have one talent, others two, and some five. The goal is not to try to do more than you can, and it's definitely not to compare yourself to someone else. Instead, the Lord expects us to be faithful and intentional about making the most with what He has given us.

Sometimes a church can be struggling and numerically small but still very much in the center of God's will. Take, for example, the church of Philadelphia in Revelation 3. This is a church with "little strength" (3:8) and probably smaller numbers than many of the others listed in the New Testament, yet they receive no rebukes and are given more encouragement than any of the other seven churches in Revelation 2-3. God is pleased and recognizes their faithfulness, giving them commendation despite the fact there are no recorded mass conversions or dynamic stories of success that we read about.

In the following chapters, I'll address growth as part of the analogy of soil, and I will sometimes mention numeric results, but please know that not all fruit is measureable and that fruit-bearing does not always equate to attendance, size, or numbers. Bigger is not automatically better, and fruitfulness can manifest itself in many different ways. There is room in the body of Christ for cell churches, small churches, large churches, and megachurches. Our priorities are faithfulness and obedience, allowing God to produce fruit as He sees fit.

3) Much of what we consider success in ministry may not actually be healthy or God-honoring. Two passages in the Bible continually trouble me as a pastor. The first is the story of Moses striking the rock in anger. Water comes forth in spite of his disobedience (Numbers 20:7-12). The second involves the Lord's sober rebuke to the church at Sardis when He says, "You have a reputation of being alive, but you are dead" (Revelation 3:1-2).

I am convinced many modern success stories that impress us may not be significant to God, and He will expose some of what we consider church growth to be shallow and man-made. In my quiet moments, I wonder whether we've struck the rock and gotten results without really being in the middle of God's will. And I wonder whether those of us who have growing congregations and have gathered some measure of reputation are really fulfilling God's purpose or if we are just perpetuating the problem. For now the Lord is silent, but one day He will speak, and when He does, I question how much of what is considered fruit-bearing will be exposed as being "dead."

The reason I share this is because I don't want to give the impression that I believe I have all the answers or that the church I pastor has its act fully together. I struggle with the fact that my congregation is not as spiritually mature as I want us to be, and sometimes I'm at a loss to define what a successful ministry really looks and feels like.

4) This book assumes essential practices and priorities that it does not expand on. While applicable to all, this book is targeted toward church leaders and is pragmatic in nature. It assumes that there are overtly spiritual functions God calls the church to practice. For example, I do not write in detail about prayer, fasting, or worship, yet I believe these are foundational elements for any congregation.

This is a targeted work, and the principles and applications I address are not meant to replace the obvious spiritual elements of ministry—only supplement them. There are plenty of books on prayer, fasting, and faith but few regarding the importance of church culture and the role it plays in nurturing a healthy, vibrant, and effective congregation. That is the focus of this book.

So, I invite you to join me in understanding why *Dirt Matters*. As you do, I pray you will come to see how this foundational principle can help your congregation maximize its redemptive potential for God's glory.

Section 1

THE PRINCIPLE

"Listen! A farmer went out to sow his seed. As he was scattering the seed, some fell along the path, and the birds came and ate it up. Some fell on rocky places, where it did not have much soil. It sprang up quickly, because the soil was shallow. But when the sun came up, the plants were scorched, and they withered because they had no root. Other seed fell among thorns, which grew up and choked the plants, so that they did not bear grain. Still other seed fell on good soil. It came up, grew and produced a crop, some multiplying thirty, some sixty, some a hundred times."

Then Jesus said, "Whoever has ears to hear, let them hear." When he was alone, the Twelve and the others around him asked him about the parables. He told them, "The secret of the kingdom of God has been given to you. But to those on the outside everything is said in parables so that "'they may be ever seeing but never perceiving, and ever hearing but never understanding; otherwise they might turn and be forgiven!'"

Then Jesus said to them, "Don't you understand this parable? How then will you understand any parable? The farmer sows the word. Some people are like seed along the path, where the word is sown. As soon as they hear it, Satan comes and takes away the word that was sown in them. Others, like seed sown on rocky places, hear the word and at once receive it with joy. But since they have no root, they last only a short time. When trouble or persecution comes because of the word, they quickly fall away. Still others, like seed sown among thorns, hear the word; but the worries of this life, the deceitfulness of wealth and the desires for other things come in and choke the word, making it unfruitful. Others, like seed sown on good soil, hear the word, accept it, and produce a crop—some thirty, some sixty, some a hundred times what was sown.

Mark 4:3-20 (NIV)

Chapter 1

DIRT REALLY DOES MATTER

How is the soil? Is it fertile or poor? – Moses

I grew up in a town of fifty thousand people in the heart of the Midwest. By no means was I a city boy, but I wasn't from the country either. My grandparents, on the other hand—they were all country. *American Gothic* country.

As a child, I would spend a few weeks every summer visiting my grandparents' farm. It was a different world for me: tractors, feeding cattle, bb-guns, square dances, horseback rides, big lunches, and mandatory afternoon naps.

Then there was the work. Generally this involved walking the bean fields to cut out weeds and unwanted corn shoots. My grandparents' fields were flat, boring, and had few or no trees. There was no scenery except rows of crops with a few barns, houses, and gravel roads in between. An occasional car driving by and kicking up dust or the attack of a random insect was all that broke the monotony.

Other relatives of mine, a great aunt and uncle, had about two hundred acres of land that was several miles away from my grandparents' farm. Farming wasn't their primary gig, though. Their property sat next to a state park and included a nice lake for fishing, some outstanding hunting ground, a big garden, and some tillable farmland they leased out.

I had been to Uncle Grover's place multiple times over the years, but it was in my late twenties that I made a valuable observation. I was there before dawn one day on a deer-hunting adventure. That particular year the crops were in the fields later than usual, so when I trekked out to my hunting spot and sat down to wait, I was able to admire a field that was ready for harvest. Sitting on that beautiful piece of property with deep ravines, thick woods, wildlife, ponds, and flat farmland between, I thought to myself, *Man, this is some great land. I bet they get killer crops here. This land is so much better than my grandparents' place… I can't imagine how much it's worth.*

That was it. Until about fifteen years later.

My great uncle and aunt had died, and I was at a gathering with some other relatives who were discussing the sale of their property. I stepped into the conversation and shared my perceived insight about how great Uncle Grover's farmland was. Another relative, who happened to be a licensed appraiser, laughed and said something like, "As far as farming goes, that land is lousy! It's composed of timber soil, which is one of the worst soils in the Midwest. They can't even plant corn there because if they do and have any kind of drought, it will die in a heartbeat. Only soybeans will grow there, and even then the land doesn't produce much of a yield."

Since I'm a preacher and, therefore, qualified to speak confidently on subjects I know absolutely nothing about, I pushed back, saying, "But when I was there hunting, I specifically remember noticing how good the field looked and thinking to myself that it had to produce an outstanding crop."

"Well," the appraiser said with a smile, "it may have looked good, but those plants didn't have many pods, and the pods that did develop had few beans— and small ones at that."

Since I'm a fast learner, I started to grasp his point, "So, you're telling me that Uncle Grover's land is not as good as my grandpa and grandma's land?"

"Not even close," he assured me.

The conversation continued for several more minutes as my relative explained to me that not only was my grandparents' land much better in quality, but also, given the same circumstances and all the same variables, their land would routinely produce twice the harvest as my Uncle Grover's land!

The same seed…
       The same fertilizers…
              The same effort…
                     The same conditions…
                            But twice the harvest!

Even if my Uncle Grover were to use extra seed, extra fertilizer, extra effort, and have optimal weather conditions, his field would still not produce the same yield as my grandparents'. Why? The answer is obvious:

Dirt matters. It really does matter.

A Much Older Story

Not all soil is the same. Each type is composed of a variety of nutrients and organic matter that accumulate in layers, called horizons. More and better nutrients and living matter produce conditions for substantially greater growth. Yet soil also varies in texture and structure based on the blended percentages of clay, silt, and sand. Too much sand and water will quickly drain through—no roots can be established, and nothing grows. Too much clay and the ground will become so hard the seed is unable to find the moisture and nutrients necessary to flourish. Too much silt and you've got nothing but mud after a hard rain, and the seed will drown.

To the untrained eye, all ground appears similar. In reality you can have two soils of significantly different quality only a short distance from one another due to variations in nutrients, matter, and texture. This may not be apparent to someone from the city, and, in some cases, it may not even be obvious to a seasoned farmer. Sometimes you have to dig down and take soil samples to really know what you've got.

Once you know what you've got, you can recognize, in turn, the potential outcomes that a field can realistically produce based upon the soil quality.

And when your livelihood is contingent upon the fruit of the land, such knowledge is a big deal.

This helps us understand why, when Moses sent spies to explore the Promised Land, he couldn't get his mind off this issue. The *first* instruction he gave the spies was, "See what the land is like" (Numbers 13:18). Then he reiterated his concern by saying, "What kind of land do they live in? Is it good or bad?" (Numbers 13:19). Finally Moses said, "How is the soil? Is it fertile or poor? Are there trees in it or not? Do your best to bring back some of the fruit of the land" (Numbers 13:20).

Think about it. After living in Egypt as slaves and then wandering in the desert where the land was poor and barren, a primary concern for Moses was the quality of the soil. He was anxious to find out what the soil in the Promised Land was like. He wanted to know if the Promised Land was going to reap a better harvest and produce a fuller crop. He wanted to know—he needed to know—is the soil good or not? Why?

Dirt matters.

A Spiritual Application

I find it interesting that Jesus used this issue of soil as the basis for one of His most popular parables. Three of the four gospels record the parable of the sower (Matthew 13; Mark 4; and Luke 8). This parable was influential enough that it was one of the few that Jesus took the time to interpret and unpack for His disciples. Living in a primarily agrarian culture, Jesus understood the basics of how soil works. He affirmed that not all soil is the same and that the same seed can produce different results if it's planted in different ground.

He linked these truths to the condition of the human heart and the ability of God's Word to produce fruit in it. When the heart/soil is hardened, shallow, or diluted, the results will be limited or non-existent. When, on the other hand, the heart/soil is fertile, amenable, and receptive, God's Word produces a great harvest. Mark's gospel says, "some thirty, some sixty, and some a hundred times what was sown" (Mark 4:20). I love that Jesus affirmed God's desire for our lives to be productive and fruitful. He wants us to yield a harvest. And notice He didn't use single digits to speak of the potential impact, but double and triple digits. Furthermore, He didn't use addition; He used multiplication to emphasize what was possible. In other words, God wants to do more in and through our lives than we can imagine.

And the key variable in this parable is—the soil. It's not about the sower. It's all about the dirt. Jesus tells us point blank that it is important to be sure that our soil is "good." Why?

Dirt matters. It really does matter.

And it matters for the community of believers as well as individual people.

Even though we think of this parable in individualistic terms, the gospel accounts of both Mark and Luke use plural terminology to make the connection between the soil and the human heart. In other words, Jesus' words apply to groups of people, not just individuals. Therefore, if the analogy of soil describes the receptivity—and, ultimately, the productivity—of God's Word in the individual's heart and life, it can also apply to the corporate community of believers.

This helps explain why you can have two churches on the same street with very similar ministries but very different outcomes. They can have comparable buildings, sincere pastors and leaders, dedicated volunteers, and even the same doctrinal bent. They can sing the same songs, have the same programs, and use the same Bible translation. Yet while one church is thriving, the other is dying. When this happens, people often shake their heads and say, "I just don't understand it."

The issue is that every church has a unique culture that serves as the soil where its ministry occurs. A church's culture is the somewhat nebulous and complex blend of norms, beliefs, attitudes, traditions, and practices that define the congregation. The culture establishes the environment that often predetermines the effectiveness or ineffectiveness of God's Word within that body of believers. It influences a congregation's potential impact more than techniques, programs, or pragmatic changes.

So, the *dogma of dirt* applies to churches as well as agriculture. Just as the quality of soil directly affects the harvest of a field and the condition of an individual's heart affects spiritual fruitfulness, a church's culture directly affects ministry outcomes. Whether we like it or not, unseen, intangible issues reside below the surface and shape the culture of a congregation, which in turn influences the potential fruit that a congregation can bear.

Failing to realize that dirt matters not only neglects a basic scriptural principle, but it also leads to frustration and disillusionment. In the process, it perpetuates a systemic problem in Western Christianity—channeling our best energy and focus into the wrong areas. So, before I flesh out church culture and how we can make it healthier, I want to highlight a primary reason churches get distracted from addressing the issue of soil quality.

Chapter 2

MISPLACED PRIORITIES

*If Esau really got his pottage in return for his birthright,
then Esau was a lucky exception. - C. S. Lewis*

A couple of things happen when your church is fortunate enough to experience rapid growth: the phone starts ringing, and your inbox starts filling up. Invariably, pastors and church leaders want to know what you're doing and if there is something they can apply to help their churches see greater results. Most of these contacts are good-hearted people who sincerely want to make a difference. They are not content with the status quo or with the thought of their churches slowly dying.

I find this encouraging. Most statistics show that four out of five congregations in America are stagnant or in decline. Some of these struggling churches don't appear too concerned while others are in denial about the fact that their congregations are slowing fading away. They seem content to go through the motions, or even if they are not content, they are hesitant to actively seek out solutions that might allow their congregations to turn around. Therefore, when someone says, "Hey, what's working? Can you give us some advice in order to help us out?" I am always anxious to help if I can.

Even as I say that, I do have a grave concern. Here's the issue: When people see what appears to be a dynamic church, they invariably focus on the visible signs of success. They look at the outward areas of ministry, which are usually issues of style, appearance, or delivery, and they attempt to replicate those:

Lights	Videos	Music
Coffee	Donuts	Foyer
Brochures	Buildings	Staffing
New Causes	New Classes	New Programs
Casual Dress	Giving Kiosk	Renaming the Church

I'm not suggesting these issues don't matter, because they do. Clearly they can carry great weight in contextualizing and communicating the gospel. For instance, if you still have 1980s clip-art on the front of your bulletin, I would fully endorse a change. Yet I fear we have succumbed to an unbalanced infatuation with issues of presentation and methodology.

If we're honest, many of us are looking for the secret sauce or the silver bullet. We attempt to oversimplify and latch onto tangible changes that give us a sense of control and an idealistic hope that we're only one decision away from turning the corner. I've been there; I know. I've gone to conferences, read books, and talked with people I respect, wanting to believe my church's problems could be easily solved with a Band-Aid or a pill. The quick fix has proved to be a myth, yet it is the predominant mindset of many churches.

Cursory Changes

Recently at a neighborhood workday, I overheard an elderly man enthusiastically talking about a project at his church. When I asked what it was about, he told me that his congregation was purchasing a new sign—a large neon one that would include a flame and a dove. He went on to tell me how his church had been over twelve-hundred people when he had started attending several decades ago but was now down to a couple hundred. This church has no young families. No kids. No passion. No life. The church is dying, and they know it. Their answer: let's buy a new sign.

I didn't have the heart to ask the question, "So, even if your new sign attracts visitors, do you think it's realistic to assume that they'll return for a second visit if you don't have any viable ministry options for them or their children?" Rather than douse his enthusiasm, I smiled and wished him well.

But this church isn't the only one to try this strategy.

I recently drove through a familiar area and passed a great church that has done some awesome ministry in their community. Yet they have been at a plateau, a predictable growth barrier, for over fifteen years now. The only way they are going to break through this barrier is by making some very difficult leadership decisions that will require courage and a change in culture. Yet as I drove by, I noticed a new church sign and a new logo—their third in the past decade.

I don't mean to sound dismissive of the sincere attempts leaders make to expand the influence of their churches. When you are on the inside, addressing such issues isn't easy. For a struggling church, any decision that will potentially cause someone to get upset and leave is scary. For a small, close-knit church, changing a ministry or program that a key member has invested in can be emotionally draining. And when your weekly offerings are barely making budget and you've got no money in the bank, a five hundred or thousand dollar decision about signs or curriculum or décor seems like a huge deal. And in many ways it is. These types of decisions do take a measure of faith, and it's commendable that churches are willing to lean into them. But make no mistake about it, in most cases they do not prove fruitful because they don't address the deeper issues.

The reality is you can change the name, the logo, the bulletin, or the dress code; you can remodel the nursery and offer free coffee and donuts, but if visitors walk into your church and sense an unhealthy culture, it really doesn't matter. You may draw people in, but you're not likely to keep them.

What worked for other congregations is irrelevant. If we don't address the culture of our churches, these cursory changes amount to little more than wasted money, wasted energy, and naïve optimism.

Good people. Good churches. Misplaced priorities.

Missing the Point

Think back to the parable of the sower. The greatest variable in Jesus' story is the soil. It is the basis for greater Kingdom impact. Jesus doesn't focus on the methods of spreading the seed or even the type of seed. His focus is all about the ground on which the seed falls. Yet when I look at the church today, I feel many of us are primarily focused on how we are distributing the seed:

Pay a hired hand?
    Use one hand or two?
        Delegate to lay planters?
            Use our left hand or right hand?
                Get the newest, flashiest, most efficient planter?
                    Purchase a spreader to plant more seeds more quickly?

While all these things can make a difference, if the soil is not healthy, the growth is going to be limited. Soil directly affects potential outcomes despite what takes place above the surface. As a result, churches need to spend more time enriching the soil, making their environment healthier, and less time looking for external, superficial fixes.

The book *The Starfish and the Spider* relates a story about a problem that hit Australia's Great Barrier Reef in the 1990s. The out of control starfish population started taking over the reef, even destroying some of the coral. A group of concerned divers took the solution into their own hands by diving down with knives and cutting the starfish in half in order to kill them.

This seemed like an easy solution, but all it did was cause the outbreak to escalate. Cutting starfish in half only causes them to generate into two new starfish. The root problem was complex. It involved rising water temperatures, a decrease in natural predators, and a change in water salinity. The solution, therefore, would not be quick and simple. It involved changing the entire culture of the reef, not just swimming down with good intentions and a knife.

Many of us are falling into the same trap. We think that because our motives are to advance God's Kingdom and because external changes or new ministry initiatives worked for someone else, those changes should work for us as well.

Like the classic analogy of an iceberg, we are tempted to focus our attention on the visible issues and miss the broader, deeper, more influential ones beneath the surface. Tweaking processes, techniques, and programs is valuable, but those things are never as important, influential, or foundational as the culture of the church.

First Things First

C.S. Lewis wrote on a couple of occasions about the failure of people to see the predictable consequences of putting second things before first things.[1] On one occasion Lewis even said that Esau was a "lucky exception" for gaining a meal in return for his birthright because the more predictable pattern is to lose both the primary and the secondary blessing as a result of putting second things before first things.

This applies to the church as well. When we prioritize the visual aspects of ministry, such as presentation and methodology (second things), we find that many of our initiatives do not work as we had hoped, and our ultimate desire of seeing real Kingdom impact never materializes. In many cases this is because we fail to give adequate attention to the deeper, more important issues of church culture and environment. We fail to address the soil and focus only on the methods of planting the seed.

Being sincere and putting effort into superficial change is simply not enough.

In the days of Micah, the people were still bringing sacrifices and offerings before the Lord, but they were neglecting the weightier matters of love, justice, and humility (Micah 6:8). As a result, the Lord told them they would plant but would not see a harvest (Micah 6:15). They were doing some good things and putting forth effort, but once again, the harvest was limited because they were failing to address the deeper issues.

Whenever we get our priorities out of order, we should not expect God's full blessing. The Lord is clear that He wants His church to produce fruit and make a redemptive difference in this world (John 15:1-16). Yet the Scriptures are equally clear that God is the one who gives the growth (1 Corinthians 3:6-8). Our job is to be faithful in doing the Lord's will. That involves planting the seed, of course, but ultimately *how* we plant is not nearly as important as *what* we plant and the soil in which it's planted.

My premise is that we have some control over the quality of soil inside the church, and focusing on that is ultimately a higher priority than just tweaking programs, activities, or creative delivery methods. But addressing soil is not easy. It's not quick, and it's definitely not flashy. As a matter of fact, when you start working with dirt, things get messy—which is why most leaders are hesitant to think about what comes next.

Chapter 3

THE KEY TO A FERTILE CULTURE

A noun is a person, place, thing, idea, or quality.

At twenty-six years old, I took over my first pastorate in a small farm town that was going through a significant transition. As the older farm families passed away, younger people from outlying areas moved in and bought their homes. Most of these new families could not afford a home in a city but could buy a less expensive one in a rural community. A few people in the church saw this as a great ministry opportunity. Others found it troubling. Their little town was changing and, in their opinion, not for the better.

When I started, the church was energized. People who had drifted returned, some wayward kids and grandkids started to visit, and a few of these "new people" dropped by. Shortly thereafter the church's youth group took their first foreign missions trip. With this wave of momentum, I called together a meeting of our leaders, singers, and musicians. I suggested that we should consider trying some new music to enhance our outreach to those in our community who were showing interest in the church.

Humbly, I began my sell: "After talking to some of our visitors, it seems that an area where we could really help our outreach as it pertains to the worship service would be adding some modern music in addition to the hymns we're singing. Let's just try one per week for a few months—nothing drastic." I was sure this would be a slam-dunk. The face of our pianist lit up; our lead singer smiled and nodded in approval, and then the organist calmly stated, "If you insist on this, then I'm going to quit." I was dumbfounded.

The leaders immediately pulled back because she was a quality musician, the organ was a sacred instrument in our church, and her husband was a leader. We continued to talk, but the conversation went nowhere. Being young and insecure, I dropped the issue.

Sometime later, I was having a casual conversation with the organist. I told her that I was building a relationship with one of the newer families in town, hoping to share Christ and get them connected to our church. She then abruptly spoke up and said, "I don't want those people coming to my church!"

And there it was in a flash; I suddenly realized that several months earlier, when I thought we had been arguing about music, we had really been arguing about values. When I thought our problem was an aspect of our worship service, the real issue involved church culture. It was about the soil.

When the congregation said they wanted to reach people, what many of them meant was that they wanted to reach a select type of person—people they already knew, liked, and loved. Some of the members wanted to reach the poor, the broken, and the lost in our community, but others were angry because they didn't want any of "those people" who were ruining their town to come in and ruin their church, too. On that day I learned something I had previously missed: our little church had much deeper issues than just song selection and the worship service. The congregation was divided over what was really most important. The dirt was bad, and the culture of our church was unhealthy.

Values are the Key

Every church has a unique culture. Whenever we visit a new congregation, we pick up subtle signs that lead us to make judgments about the nature of that church. Some elements of church culture can be observed in the external environment, such as the décor, the dress code, the average age, and the energy or lack thereof. All these factors send signals that we quickly receive.

Yet the more critical elements of church culture are not easily observed. More than architecture, relevant programming, glossy bulletins, or matching t-shirts, every local church has distinguishing characteristics that influence who that congregation is and what is important to them. These subtle influencers can be called principles, traits, qualities, or characteristics, but they are really values—commonly held beliefs within a church that affect attitudes and actions. There are few things that influence the culture of a congregation more than its values.

Unfortunately, the term "values" can be one of those words that we use all the time without fully grasping its meaning and importance. The best definition that I've come across is this: "The core of what your organization is and what your organization cherishes. Values are traits or qualities that are considered worthwhile; they represent an individual's highest priorities and deeply held driving forces and beliefs."[2] Here are a few additional characteristics of values:

- They are guiding principles that provide direction.
- They influence conduct, behavior, activity, and mission.
- They help determine how things will be done.
- They provide a foundation for discerning what is most important.
- They are passionately believed and emotionally owned.

Not This

Values, therefore, are important characteristics that not only reflect, but also sway and mold a church's culture. But they must be real, believed, and lived out. To simply have a list of values without praxis doesn't accomplish anything. Sometimes churches, businesses, and organizations develop values, but they don't really own them, believe them, or emphasize them.

One of the funeral homes in our area has their mission, vision, and core values framed on the wall. Their list of values includes integrity, respect, excellence, and enduring relationships. The problem is that I don't see or feel many of these when I work with the funeral home. These values sound great, but they don't reflect the culture of that business. In reality the building is outdated; the carpet is worn; the sound system is poor; the office is messy, and the copier is awful. Yet one of the values on the wall is "excellence." The real value that is modeled and portrayed in that business is profit. It's about saving a buck, making the sale, and meeting the quota for the corporation. But "we value excellence," sounds so much better than "we value profit."

In the case of this funeral home and in the case of many churches, the list of values developed does not reflect reality. One of the reasons this happens is because leaders go to a conference or read a book that tells them they ought to create a list of values. Or they notice that other organizations they respect have a list of values, so they seek to develop their list, but they don't understand *why* this is important. Therefore, they end up with a list of values that sound spiritual and good, but aren't really true. Unfortunately, when values are developed in this way, the result is often a list of five, seven, or ten admirable words or phrases that don't really have much of an effect.

The first time I was challenged to develop core values, I went to one of the most influential churches in America for a one-day workshop where one of the teaching pastors was parroting the senior minister's material on the subject. I was a little overwhelmed, and during a break I approached the speaker and asked, "How do you define values?" She looked at me and said, "I don't know; I'll have to ask." I appreciated her honesty, but it was troubling that the person who had just been teaching me the importance of this topic didn't have a great grasp of it either. I left the workshop feeling like I needed to develop a list of values for our church, but I had no idea what I was doing or why I was doing it.

Once I was home, I hit the websites of dozens of churches, raking through their value statements to find the ones I liked. The elders and I carved that list down to seven, and then—boom—we had core values! The trouble was we didn't own them. We didn't live them. We didn't emphasize them. Some of the values reflected our church, but others did not. We lacked symmetry between what we had on paper and who we were as a congregation.

Much like the funeral home, one of our values was excellence, but the quality of our building, the expectations of our leaders, and the content within many of our ministries pointed toward faithfulness and sincerity more than excellence. By having excellence listed as a value, we were kidding ourselves, and we were losing credibility with people who saw the discontinuity between what we said and what we actually did.

When I talk about values, I'm not talking about a contrived list of words that are put together because that's the thing to do; I'm talking about the characteristics that help define the very nature and help share the entire environment of your church. These qualities are believed in passionately and considered of paramount importance. They are *not* sterile statements, wishful intentions, or half-hearted beliefs.

Think Nouns

One of the important things to keep in mind about values is that they are nouns. Churches are infatuated with verbs and for good reason. The church *should* be about action and mission. But nouns are essential, too. A noun is a person, place, thing, idea, or quality. Nouns speak about substance, not action, even though they influence action. This is important because soil is a noun! Soil is not an action—it's a substance—yet it forms the context in which the seed grows and produces fruit.

While our natural inclination is to think of values in terms of action (verbs), we need to begin understanding them as nouns. To illustrate, the book of Nehemiah says, "the joy of the Lord is your strength" (Nehemiah 8:10). Generally, when most people preach this passage, they communicate the importance of being joyful, and they usually include several applications on *how* to be more joyful. But here's the issue: if you look at that passage, the word "joy" is a noun. Nehemiah wasn't telling the people to *try* being joyful so they could be stronger in the Lord. He was telling them to go celebrate Passover, focus on the Lord for who He is and what He's done, and, as a result, to expect that God would give them a state of joy and a measure of strength. This is a much different emphasis than telling people to smile more, think positive thoughts, and all the other things we try to do in order to generate joy.

We often do the same thing with the fruit of the Spirit in Galatians. We tend to teach and preach these nine qualities as verbs or actions that we are to manufacture as good Christians. But in reality, they are all nouns, character traits that are to be naturally evident rather than produced in our lives. The Apostle Paul isn't saying, "Work hard at being more gentle so you're doing what God wants you to do." He's saying, "*Walk* in the Spirit, and crucify your flesh." As a result, God will transform your character and make you a gentler, Christ-centered person in the core of your being.

I'm not suggesting that it's a sin to apply Nehemiah 8:10 or Galatians 5 as actions. Clearly the Bible uses joy and gentleness as both verbs and nouns. Sometimes they are actions that we are commanded to do, but ultimately, they are character traits that should be manifested in our lives. An action is something done out of good motives or bad. A character trait reveals who we are. There's a big difference between being a jerk who does an isolated act of grace and a gracious person who consistently does gracious acts because that's who he or she is.

That's why when I talk about values, I'm talking about nouns—characteristics that reflect who the members of the congregation are, not just isolated things they are going to do. Values are defining qualities that help us to understand who we are as a church body, or at least who we are aspiring to be.

Categories of Manifestation

Values profoundly affect church culture. As a result, they provide the nutrients that help influence the quality of the soil. The depth to which those values are embedded into the heart of the congregation further determines quality and health.

I'll be sharing five values consistent with a healthy church culture in the second section of this book. I call these five values *Activators*. They enhance the culture of any church that emphasizes them. Nonetheless, there is room for variance in the number and specific values individual congregations embrace.

Just like farmland, there is no one soil makeup, or mixture of values, that is perfect for every church. This can be illustrated by the farmland found in my state. In Illinois, there are over seven hundred specific soil types that are traditionally grouped into three subsets or classifications. Class A soils are the best. They provide the healthiest environment for growth to occur. Farmers can expect a harvest of 200 or more bushels of corn per acre with Class A soil. Class B is still considered good soil, and one can expect 140 bushels and up. Class C soil is of a much lower quality, though. In some cases, an acre may not even yield 100 bushels. Within each of these categories, there are literally dozens, and in some cases, hundreds of specific soil types that vary greatly in minerals, texture, and organic matter.

While every church should seek the Lord to determine what mixture of values He is moving them to embody, I find that, much like the soils of Illinois, there are three general categories in which values are played out in a local church. There are obviously various levels of health and fluctuation within each of these categories, but as a general rule, these hold true:

Fragmented Values

When a congregation lacks unity in their value system and actually has competing principles and ideologies at work, they have fragmented values. These values are diffused, and there is no strong consensus about what is important, how to do things, why things are done, etc. Mainline churches that have a division between conservatives and liberals contending for power serve as a great example. These churches have two extreme, passionately held worldviews seeking control because of their core convictions. Churches like these can survive and exist for a period of time, but there's a reason many are dying and splitting.

This is unhealthy soil, and it provides an environment in which the fruitfulness of God's Word is going to be limited. Yes, there will still be isolated stories of life-change, but these churches know deep down in their hearts that they are not reaching their redemptive potential. The soil is bad because the value system is fragmented.

Even within conservative, Bible-believing churches that have a mission statement on the wall and use their doctrinal statement as bookmarks, the value system can still be fragmented. Let's say that half of the church board holds to an unwritten opinion that the traditions of the church are just as important as the Scriptures. The other half of the board holds to an unwritten belief that traditions don't really matter. This church is unified in doctrine and mission, but it's only a matter of time before an issue arises that exposes the unhealthy culture that is dormant in the church board. The church may appear healthy on the surface, but fragmented values indicate that the soil is of poor quality, which will eventually result in predictable problems and limited fruit.

Unified, Unhealthy Values

When a congregation has complete unity in doctrine, purpose, and values but their value system consists of unhealthy principles and practices, they have unified, unhealthy values. The small church from Kansas that pickets funerals, protests against Jews and gays, and publicly thanks God for natural disasters is a good example. They are completely unified in what they believe and hold true, and their beliefs drive their actions. Yet the values they display are a poor reflection of the love and grace of God. The soil is beyond bad—it's toxic.

A less extreme example is the struggling church that has seen a fifty percent decline in attendance over the past decade, has no missional presence in the community, yet is completely unified in their belief that they don't have to change anything. They have people serving outside of their giftedness; they insist on doing church like it was done one hundred years ago, and the only reasons they can come up with for their decreasing attendance are that people aren't committed anymore and that the only churches that are growing are compromising the gospel. They have unified beliefs, but those beliefs are rooted in myths, bad leadership, and self-righteous denial. That equals bad soil.

Unified, Healthy Values

When a congregation has a critical mass of people who hold to a common set of scriptural principles which govern what they do and how they do it, they can be classified as having unified, healthy values. Unified, healthy values are biblically consistent values that may be written or unwritten; they may be consciously or unconsciously held. They are present in the hearts of the leadership and a majority of the people. When a church has unified, healthy values consistently in place, their culture is healthier, and their potential Kingdom influence is enhanced.

At a meeting in Dallas, Texas, I listened to Pastor Toby Slough from Cross Timbers Community Church tell the story about transitioning his congregation into one of the most generous churches in America. For Cross Timbers Community Church, generosity is not just a program or an isolated initiative; it is a value that is being emphasized and lived out. As a result, during a time when the church was running at a shortfall, they decided to give away almost all the money they had in their reserve fund. On another occasion, people were told they could take money *out* of the offering as it was passed if they had a pressing need. In addition, the church gave away their entire Christmas offering one year. Through all of this, not only were people being blessed and God was being glorified, but also the amount of money given to the church continued to increase.

These types of stories aren't just coincidence. They are the result of the body of Christ coming together around common values and then acting in faith to live them out. When this happens, God blesses, and the church's potential influence increases exponentially.

Specific Results

It can be tempting to ignore the hard work of articulating values in favor of simpler, more superficial changes, especially in our action-oriented world of quick-fix solutions. However, when you understand the *dogma of dirt*, you realize values are worth addressing.

In his book *Advanced Strategic Planning*, Aubrey Malphurs notes that dynamic ministries almost always have people with shared values. He also says churches that are struggling often have confusion and discontinuity in basic values.[3] Furthermore, my experience has allowed me to see firsthand a number of tangible benefits associated with churches that have unified, healthy values in place.

- *Unified, Healthy Values build continuity.* Church consultant and seasoned author Lyle Schaller says that a clash in values is the number one source of conflict in churches and the main reason for disagreements over priorities and goals.[4] The opposite is also true.

When a church has unified, healthy values, it usually has greater continuity and internal harmony.

- *Unified, Healthy Values help determine what's most important.* Most churches struggle to set their priorities in terms of ministries, budgets, programs, etc. Values help determine what is best for each specific body of believers, and those values become a grid to determine and evaluate what really matters most. Without unified, healthy values, most churches have no foundation to determine what's most important. Therefore, they default to a personality, a squeaky wheel, tradition, or what they read in a book or heard at a conference.

- *Unified, Healthy Values clarify who is going to stay and who needs to leave.* When the values are clear, owned, and practiced, it becomes easier for people to sense whether they belong or not—or whether they want to belong or not. We don't want to lose anyone, but sometimes people need to move on for both their sake and the church's. Unified, healthy values help people see whether they really fit with a church or not.

- *Unified, Healthy Values expedite and streamline decision-making.* Roy Disney once said, "It's not hard to make decisions when you know what your values are." When leadership teams work to develop unified, healthy values, they find that decisions come more quickly and easily, and those decisions are usually better ones at that.

- *Unified, Healthy Values inspire loyalty and action.* When a congregation defines and, more importantly, lives out their values, they will attract people who share those values. Those who buy in to those unified, healthy values have greater ownership of the church and will be more likely to get involved and contribute in some measure. Commitment runs much deeper than just a response to an inspired sermon or an emotional plea.

- *Unified, Healthy Values help people address conflict in a more spiritually mature way.* I have found that even when people disagree with a decision, they are more likely to do so in a mature, civil, and non-personal way when they are in sync with the values, mission, and vision of a church. Conflict will always occur, and obviously there will be exceptions, but when people believe in who you are and what you are doing, there is enough common ground to maintain trust and perspective in spite of frustrations over isolated issues.

- *Unified, Healthy Values help maintain momentum.* A sure sign of bad church culture and fragmented values is a loss of momentum whenever the congregation seems to be moving forward. Whenever optimism builds, a problem arises that brings things to a halt. There will always be challenges, but congregations with solid values tend to push through and keep moving forward in spite of setbacks.

- *Unified, Healthy Values promote greater confidence in the leadership.* When people know what you stand for and realize that you are sincere and committed to the values you proclaim, it enhances credibility and trust. They are less likely to question your motives because they know who you are, what you stand for, and why you are doing what you're doing.

Dirt matters. And healthy values embedded in the collective consciousness of the church body provide the fertile soil in which God's Word is released to bear fruit in and through the church. The size and scope of fruit is God's concern, but if we can nurture the soil in order to make the culture of the church healthier, we must. And, contrary to what some people think, the quality of the soil can be changed.

Chapter 4

ENHANCING THE QUALITY

*The seed falling on good soil refers to people who
hear the word and understand it.* – Jesus

After six and a half years at my first church, I accepted a call to become the Lead Pastor of Richwoods Christian Church in Peoria, Illinois. This thirty-year-old congregation had always been a single-cell church where everyone knew everyone, and when a visitor showed up on a Sunday morning, well, everyone knew we had a visitor. The congregation was composed of some great people who were sincere in their faith, did good works, and had a genuine desire to see people impacted by the gospel. But while they had some success stories, they had never come close to tapping their Kingdom potential. They knew it. The interim minister knew it. I knew it.

When I came for my interview, I was upfront with the board, search committee, and congregation about my philosophy of ministry and the types of changes I felt the congregation would need to make. I would push the church to a commitment of reaching the lost to the point that everything would be evaluated and potentially changed or modified that was not explicitly biblical in nature.

I wanted to stress the importance of "second things," such as issues of presentation and methodology, letting them know that our church was going to lean into them, while simultaneously giving them a realistic expectation of what they were going to get if they hired me. That way they could not say I oversold myself or gave them a bait-and-switch.

Even though I had informed the congregation that we were going to shake things up, I knew we weren't going to do so quickly. The Lord had spoken to me clearly that Richwoods needed a change in culture before we changed the forms and programs. So, I had resolved to address the soil before addressing the externals. Fortunately, through prayer, the Holy Spirit, and a great group of people around me, we were able to see the culture changed and the soil enhanced. As a result, the impact of our church far exceeded anything we could have imagined just a few years ago.

Some people take a fatalistic view of existing churches. They would have us believe that it's too hard for small and dying churches to be resurrected and we should channel all our energy and resources into planting new ones. "After all," they say, "it's easier to have a baby than to raise the dead." Well, I'm all for church planting, but I also believe in resurrections. And while new babies are amazing, there is something utterly unique and awe-inspiring about a resurrection.

If we change the soil, resurrections can happen. Languishing, struggling, and dying churches can be turned around—brought back to life. They can even go places they've never gone before. But, it's *not* easy. It's a process, and it takes commitment. Actually, it takes three nonnegotiable commitments in order to enhance the quality of existing soil.

A Commitment to Good Content

First of all, we must commit to nurturing the right values into the culture of the church in order to enhance its quality. In agriculture it is well known that not all soil is the same. Even ground that is considered Class A, high-quality, high-yielding soil can still vary greatly in topsoil, structure, nutrients, and organic matter. In fact, there are multiple soil types that can provide thriving environments for growth, even though they look different, feel different, and are different in substance and makeup. They are still excellent in quality, but far from identical.

The same is true for churches. There is no *one* culture or list of values that is right for every congregation. As a result, there is no formula to be copied. There are dozens of values that are biblical, healthy, galvanizing, and true (see Appendix I). When these values are injected into the heart of the congregation, they serve as a fertile environment for God's Word to flourish and bear fruit.

> There is no *one* list.
> There is no *complete* list.
> There is no *perfect* list.

Church leaders must seek the Lord and His Word to discover the right blend of values for their body of believers. Leaders need to take soil samples to determine what is present and what needs to be injected into the ground in order to make it healthier. These values must be conscious, owned, and, at the very least, implied. If they are defined in writing, it is even better, but they must be reflected in the vocabulary, actions, and hearts of the people.

Actual versus Aspirational

One of the key insights for fostering good content is to make a distinction between a church's actual values and aspirational values. Actual values are the traits and principles that a church truly holds to, whether they are defined, promoted, and recognized or not. A church needs to understand what their actual values are and then build on those values or, in some cases, begin to shift the church away from those values if they are unhealthy.

Aspirational values, on the other hand, are what you want or hope to become but currently are not. It is important to clarify the difference because injecting new values into a congregation is, in many ways, identifying aspirational values and working to make them actual ones. But this takes time. If you simply start talking about aspirational values as if they are actual values, you will lose credibility and undermine the entire process.

For example, one should not say that authenticity is a core value of the church unless it really is. Unless that congregation is modeling a measure of relational transparency in their struggles, sins, and temptations, then authenticity is probably not an actual value. If people hear the leadership talking about how important authenticity is but they don't see it in action, they can become cynical. The better course is for the leaders to simply identify authenticity as an aspirational value. They should then be upfront with the congregation, explaining that, though this value is not being presently lived out in the church, they are committed to making it a priority moving forward.

When I started at Richwoods, I tried to ask questions, make observations, and pray for discernment until it became evident to me that there were clear *value-gaps*—issues below the surface—that negatively affected the culture of our congregation. For example, some of the core members did not have a good theological grasp of biblical change and, as a result, still had a hard time understanding the difference between methodology (forms and traditions of ministry) and the message (truth of Scripture). Therefore, the leadership made the principle of biblical change an aspirational value that we were committed to instilling into the consciousness of our church. We had to teach on this, model it, illustrate it, and clarify it, until a majority of our people clearly understood how to differentiate between the methods and the message.

Another example involved the fact that many in our church had an idealistic view of growth and outreach. They wanted to reach people and were very committed to foreign missions, but they had virtually no relationships with non-Christians. They were naïve when it came to understanding the mindsets of the unchurched and lacked experience in how to connect and share their faith with the average unbeliever. So, I took the existing congregational value of outreach and redefined and deepened it into the heart of the church. By expanding the congregation's understanding of outreach and by emphasizing the importance of making the gospel relevant, I was shifting the mindset of our congregation and enhancing the quality of the soil.

Primary versus Secondary

Another key element of good content is to understand the tensions that can arise between biblical values. When these tensions appear, we must have some sense of how to navigate them. Otherwise, we can have a list of values that causes confusion and frustration and becomes counter-productive.

A biblical example can be found in 1 Corinthians 14, where the Apostle Paul challenges the church about using the gift of tongues in the worship service, especially when non-believers are present. Paul emphasizes the fact that he's glad people have that gift and are using it. Yet he prioritizes clarity, order, instruction, and sensitivity to the unbeliever over the unrestrained use of tongues in the public worship service. He's not condemning tongues, but he is saying that it's secondary to these other concerns in that context.

A more modern and practical example is the tension between authenticity and quality. Both of these elements of worship are important and have biblical merit, yet sometimes they clash. Having someone who is sincere but not necessarily gifted sing a heartfelt worship song can be a blessing. Other times, it can cause people to cringe and leave visitors running for the door. But we can also prioritize quality to the point that arrogance settles in and waves of capable people are marginalized and shamed because they aren't good enough.

If a congregation is not aware of these tensions, they may be talking about or even attempting to practice healthy biblical values only to find they are experiencing more conflict and disunity as a result. Part of developing good content is understanding that tensions will occur and then developing a consistent way of determining what values trump others.

Individual versus Organizational

Finally, it is important to understand the difference between individual values and organizational values. Every individual has personal values, and sometimes it is easy to project those onto the entire church body. This is especially true for leaders and groups of people in the church who share similar convictions. If they are not careful, they can falsely assume the entire church values what they value, or at least the entire church *should* value what they value. This attitude almost always leads to problems.

For example, if one group of people within the church believes teaching is the primary function of the body, another group believes it is missions, and a third group believes it is public worship, then conflict can occur. Without even realizing it, each group can assume their biblical value is most important and that everyone else agrees, should agree, or will eventually agree. Even though each group embraces a healthy, biblical value, the convictions of the three groups will inevitably clash and pull the church in different directions.

Therefore, it is imperative that you learn to distinguish your personal values and the values of sub-groups within your church from overall congregational values. Much like a middle school math student looking for the common denominator among a group of fractions, you must find the common values of your church body among the individual values of members.

Ultimately, good content, or the right mix of values, is essential to developing a healthy church culture. And in order to have that, you must grasp the disparity between actual and aspirational, primary and secondary, and individual and organizational values. In doing so, you put yourself in a position to determine the right values for your church and thereby enhance the soil quality.

A Commitment to Intentionality

Introducing the right content can change the culture of your church, but this will not happen accidentally. You will not stumble across it or wave a magic wand and make it happen. You must thoughtfully, consistently, and purposefully work to make new values stick. As Steven Covey states, "Anything less than a conscious commitment to the important is an unconscious commitment to the unimportant."[5]

Leaders get busy doing ministry—taking phone calls, doing crisis intervention, assimilating new people, making hospital calls, and preparing for lessons—to the point that they don't think about or prioritize such things as values. When this busyness is coupled with the pressure to succeed and the guilt we feel when we compare ourselves to the church down the street, we really don't feel as though we have the time to do this. We need results *now*. So, we pour ourselves into the urgent. But what is most urgent is not always most important. And even if we know what's important, it takes a great deal of courage and focus to address it.

In my first church, most of the men on the board were also members of the Masonic Lodge. They assured me that this was no cause for concern. I had no doubt that these men where Christian guys who loved the Lord, but I also felt that, when push came to shove, they were more committed to their lodge brothers than they were to their church brothers. Once again, this is a values issue—one that I chose to ignore.

Everything was fine for a while. The first sign of trouble came when we prepared to purchase a new sound system. A new attendee at our church was helping me research and look for options. We found a solid system at a wonderful price. But one of the lodge members, who knew nothing about sound, decided we needed a different type of system and took it upon himself to seek out options. I didn't understand why until some time later when I found out that the lodge member had a longstanding issue with the new attendee who was helping me. Ultimately, the church spent over twice the money we should have for a poor sound system because one lodge member didn't like the guy who was helping and the rest of the church board wanted to support their lodge brother.

And the consequences didn't stop with a poor financial decision. Several months later, the same lodge member, angry over a business deal from years earlier, physically attacked the new attendee in a public place yelling, "I don't want you coming to my church!" Then he tackled the man and began punching him. I felt alone in addressing the issue because most of the men on the church board didn't want to confront their lodge brother.

Truthfully, most of the men on the church board were good guys who were committed to the church. They treated my wife and me wonderfully. But, at the end of the day, they had divided loyalties. You could see it in their eyes and hear in their voices when certain issues arose. The women knew it. The men who didn't belong to the lodge knew it. But the guys who were lodge members refused to acknowledge it. And I lacked the courage to address it.

When we don't have the nerve or the focus to be intentional about addressing the value gaps in the church, we may get by for a while, but ultimately, we are planting our seed in poor soil, and we are limiting the church. We usually find that we are spinning our wheels, dealing with one crisis after another, bouncing from optimism to pessimism, and shaking our heads in disbelief over the discontinuity and challenges that we are dealing with internally and externally. We find that everything is harder and less productive without good soil.

There are really only four ways to get good soil. One, we get lucky and stumble upon it. Two, we diligently search for it, and when we find it, we jump on it. Three, God supernaturally leads us to it like He did the Israelites. Or four, we develop it. We take what we have, and we nurture it, enrich it, and transform it into a higher quality. But doing this takes more than a sermon series, a program, a retreat, a class, or a congregational meeting. We must emphasize soil development systematically.

The third section of this book will give specific steps on how to do this. For now, realize that once we see the value gaps in the church and we understand the values that need to be cultivated, we must intentionally and purposefully work to nurture those values into the heart of our churches. Then, there is one more commitment we must make.

A Commitment to Time

Shortly before I moved to Peoria, I came across a quote from Rick Warren in which he said that it only takes eight feet for a rowboat to make a U-turn, but it takes an oil tanker at least fourteen miles. He added that too many pastors treat the church like a rowboat, when in reality it's a big ship. This left an impression on me, and over the years I've come to believe it is even more accurate than I initially believed.

Changing the culture of an existing church is not a quick fix, and if we think an awesome sermon or even a good series is going to do it, we're woefully mistaken. Regardless of how amazing the preaching or content is, it takes time to change culture. Almost every consultant and author that I've come across says that it takes a minimum of three to four years to transition the culture of an existing organization.[6] My observation is that, unless you have a very strong leadership at the helm, it is more likely to take five to ten years when dealing with a church.

The reason it takes longer to change the culture of an existing church as compared to a business is because the church is a volunteer-intensive organization, and there are no incentives such as salaries, bonuses, or benefits to entice people. The church is also dealing with tradition and tapping into people's deepest convictions, which don't usually change easily. On top of all this, we've only got access to people a few hours each week, and even then, they are usually worn down from their personal lives, so they don't have the emotional energy to wrestle with paradigm shifts and value systems.

Much like planning for retirement, changing church culture is a long-term task. It takes time to nurture the soil and allow values to soak into the heart and consciousness of the people. If we go too quickly, not only will we end up disappointed, we may even end up like my father-in-law's front yard. He over-fertilized one spring and, due to the abundance of nitrogen, wound up with brown strips. Even though his intention was a lush, green yard, he scorched it for an entire year.

Fortunately, my father-in-law's yard bounced back. Sometimes churches don't.

God's view of fruit-bearing differs from our cultural expectation of having immediate and measurable results. We need to step back, slow down, work the soil, enrich the land, and trust God. In 2 Kings 19:29-30, the Lord told Hezekiah, "This year you will eat what grows by itself, and the second year what springs from that. But in the third year sow and reap, plant vineyards and eat their fruit. Once more a remnant of the house of Judah will take root below and bear fruit above." Notice what God told Hezekiah: the seeds will take root below the surface, and you'll enjoy fruit. Ultimately it will take three years before you see a true harvest! God wanted to bless Hezekiah with abundant fruit, but it wasn't going to come in one day, one month, or even one year. It was going to be a process that involved time and patience.

Before this, in the days of Moses, the Lord spoke to the people and said, "When you plant a fruit tree, do not eat the fruit for three years, consider it forbidden. The fourth year shall be an offering to the Lord, but in the fifth you may eat… in this way your harvest will be increased" (Lev 19:23-25). God called them to *trust Him*, and, as they obeyed and waited, He promised them an increased harvest. Yet they could not expect to see the outcome they dreamed of until year *five*! Such a mentality flies in the face of our modern desire for immediate results, which is why we focus so much energy on the wrong things.

Thankfully, this was a message God laid on my heart, and by His grace I was able to heed it. As a result, my primary goal when I came to Richwoods was to take the necessary time to influence the culture of the church by instilling healthy values rather than getting a better building or reworking all of our programs. Yes, we made changes, but more than that, we focused on shaping the culture by cultivating unified, healthy values. And God blessed it.

The same is true for my friend Tim Harlow, who pastors Parkview Christian Church in Orland Park on the Southside of Chicago. When he came to Parkview, the church was 40 years old and was averaging 150 in attendance. After five years, the church grew to 250. After ten years, attendance was 500. Their numeric growth was solid, but more importantly, the church was taking on a new identity and a healthier culture. Tim was guiding the congregation to embrace a new set of values, a new vision, and a new mission. Today, Parkview is running almost 7000 people in weekly attendance and has been featured as one of the fastest growing churches in America.

While Tim's story may be an extreme example, the principle holds true. The bottom line is this: it only takes a day to change a program and a few weeks to remodel a building, but it takes years to change culture. Yet when the culture tips, becoming healthy and vibrant, the potential impact of the church goes up immeasurably.

The "Get It" Factor

Changing culture requires good content, intentionality, and time. As these three commitments are made, the collective heart of the congregation is likely to become more open and receptive to God's Word and God's will. As a result, the church is put into a position where the Lord is able to move and work in a way that maximizes the congregation's redemptive potential.

In the parable of the sower, Jesus defines the good soil as the "people who hear the word and understand it" (Matthew 13:23). The Greek word for "understand" is *suvieis*, which means to comprehend, discern, be aware, or have insight into. A more modern definition might be "getting it." That's really what it means. It's when people hear the written and the living Word of God and are able to "get it" to the point that they can grasp what God is saying and apply it beyond the superficial. As a result, the seed takes root and grows in and through us, yielding an abundant harvest for God's glory (Colossians 1:6). That's the good soil.

Another interesting fact about the usage of *suvieis* in this passage is that it's a present active participle. It is a continuous action, *not* a fixed or one-time event. This teaching is not just about people receiving the gospel and becoming Christians; it's also about the never-ending, continual activity of having open and receptive hearts.

Part of our job is to help facilitate and nurture an environment in which the local church is able to better hear and understand God's Word and will. When we enhance the quality of the soil, we are helping people to "get it," and we are putting the church and ourselves in a position to bear much fruit.

Because "hearing and understanding" is a continual process, good soil can be corrupted and become bad soil. Conversely, bad soil can be transitioned into good soil. If the soil is poor and needs to be enhanced, it takes a commitment to good content, intentionality, and time. Those three things are non-negotiable. They simply must be embraced in order to transform the culture of a church.

Too often, pastors and church leaders become fatalistic and write a church off when enriching the soil proves too difficult or takes too long. They bounce to a new congregation with new hopes and dreams, only to be disappointed again. Sometimes we do need to move on. The soil is so bad that it simply can't be changed. But don't write off existing churches too quickly. More often than we think, the soil can be modified. And when the soil is changed and people begin to "get it," amazing things can happen!

Section 2

THE ACTIVATORS

The term *Activators* describes key values that serve as catalysts in developing a healthier church culture. These values are essential in establishing an environment that is consistent with good soil. When they are in place, they increase the likelihood that other values will stick and that the church will become healthier, vibrant, and more effective in carrying out its mission.

Chapter 5

GENUINE DEPENDENCE

"God invites us to take a holiday, to stop being God for a while, and let Him be God." - Simon Tugwell

After 15 years of ministry, I hit a wall. I had great people in my life and a thriving church that I loved. Yet internally I was empty and scared.

One day as I was reflecting upon the disconnect between an externally successful ministry and my internal angst, the thought occurred to me, *I can do this without Jesus. I have the giftedness and the drive, and I've gained enough experience that I can produce short-term results without needing Christ.*

I don't mean to be offensive, but, when that thought crossed my mind, it scared the hell out of me.

Not only did I realize that thought was wrong, but I knew that my internal struggle was likely going to lead me down one of several paths. One, I would implode under the pressure of making ministry happen by my own strength. Two, I might do something stupid or leave the ministry in an attempt to escape the stress. Three, I would just lose my heart and become a professional minister, doing my job but not really giving my heart and soul to Christ or His people. Four, I would view this as a wake-up call, an opportunity to recapture my first love.

Fortunately, with the help of solid people and a powerful retreat in Colorado, I was able to reconnect with Jesus in a way that I hadn't in several years.[7] My passion for Christ and for His calling upon my life was resurrected in a newfound way. As a result, I was able to refocus on a core lesson that I once held dear but had begun to neglect over time: the importance of being fully reliant upon God.

When I started in ministry, I knew that I was unqualified, in over my head, and had no business doing what I was doing. I didn't have many answers—only questions. I would get so nervous before funerals that I could hardly talk due to cottonmouth, and I literally had no clue what to say or do in a majority of my counseling appointments. The only thing I had to offer was Christ working through me. Daily I would submit to Him, acknowledging my inadequacy and confessing my need for God to work through my weakness.

Over time and with a little success, I subtly began to do ministry on autopilot. I fell into the danger zone of thinking I could actually do it. My prayers of dependence became fewer and fewer as I grew in wisdom and experience. Don't get me wrong. I would still pray, worship, and do devotions, and I was sincere in my desire to help people for God's glory. Yet deep in my heart I had become self-sufficient. For some reason it was just easier for me to take control and do things myself than it was to seek God, trust Him, and then do it with Him. Gradually and unintentionally, I began to marginalize Christ, and I trusted more in myself than in Jesus.

Even though God has opened my eyes to this sinful pattern of behavior and I have begun to trust in Him again in a new way, I find that it's still a struggle. I still tend to trust more in myself than in Him. I don't think my story is unique.

What God Desires

The Lord longs for His people, and His shepherds in particular, to abandon our pride, independence, and need for control. To surrender ourselves, trusting Him to work in and through us to do that which we cannot do ourselves. To humble ourselves, believing that even the things we can do, we can't really do without Christ (John 15:5). To have a heartfelt reliance upon Him for strength, guidance, wisdom, provisions, courage, and growth. As the saying goes, "~~God doesn't help those who help themselves; He helps those who admit they're helpless.~~"

This is not to say we should be passive.

David was assertive when he picked up the five stones and went out to face Goliath. Yet as he went, he boldly stated, "You come against me with sword and spear and javelin, but I come against you in the name of the Lord Almighty… This day the Lord will deliver you into my hands" (1 Samuel 17:45-46). David was responsible and active yet grounded in absolute trust.

The Lord told Zerubbabel he was responsible for completing the reconstruction of the temple, but also told him, "It's not by might, nor by power, but by my Spirit" (Zechariah 4:6,8). God didn't magically drop the temple from heaven. He called Zerubbabel to make it happen, but even as he commissioned Zerubbabel for service, the Lord reminded him it was the Spirit working through him that was going to get the job done.

When God called Gideon, He referred to him as a mighty warrior, but Gideon replied, "Pardon me, my Lord, but how can I save Israel? My clan is the weakest in Manasseh, and I am the least in my family. The Lord answered, 'I will be with you'" (Judges 6:15-16). Then God took this scared, hesitant, doubting man, stripped his troops down from several thousand to three hundred, and brought victory. Why? So Israel would not say, "Our own strength has saved us" (Judges 7:2).

The Apostle Paul was a courageous and bold leader, yet he acknowledged, "I will boast all the more gladly about my weaknesses, so that Christ's power may rest on me. That is why, for Christ's sake, I delight in weaknesses, in insults, in hardships, in persecutions, in difficulties. For when I am weak, then I am strong" (2 Corinthians 12:9-10).

Yes, we are to take initiative. We are to be active. It's okay to plan and prepare. Yet we are ultimately to trust that Jesus is the one building His church and He is merely using us as conduits (Matthew 16:28). As the Psalmist wrote, "Unless the Lord builds the house, the builders labor in vain. Unless the Lord watches over the city, the guards stand watch in vain" (Psalm 127:1).

One of the most eloquent and passionate prayers of dependence I've ever read is ascribed to St. Patrick, a dedicated, zealous, and highly successful missionary. This prayer gets to the heart of God because it shows diligence in mission, yet genuine reliance upon the Lord.

I arise today
Through God's strength to pilot me;
God's might to uphold me,
God's wisdom to guide me,
God's eye to look before me,
God's ear to hear me,
God's word to speak for me,
God's hand to guard me,
God's way to lie before me,
God's shield to protect me,
God's hosts to save me
Afar and anear,
Alone or in a multitude.
Christ shield me today.

Christ with me, Christ before me, Christ behind me,
Christ in me, Christ beneath me, Christ above me,
Christ on my right, Christ on my left,
Christ when I lie down, Christ when I sit down,
Christ in the heart of everyone who thinks of me,
Christ in the mouth of everyone who speaks of me,
Christ in the eye that sees me,
Christ in the ear that hears me.
I arise today
Through the mighty strength
Of the Lord of creation.

God desires genuine prayers of dependence and surrender, not trite prayers of submission out of obligation, nor prayers of petition that we toss up with the goal of manipulating God. The Lord wants us to be fully dedicated to the work He calls us to and to pursue this work with humility and reliance.

When we rely upon God, we are more likely to carry out ministry with the *peace* of Christ, feeling less pressure to measure up and compare ourselves to others. Then we are not striving out of an unhealthy ambition but tackling ministry at a *pace* more in step with Jesus, who was never hurried or rushed. We are more *patient* and obedient to wait on God and His timing. I find the more dependent I am, the more I *pray* out of a place of desire rather than duty. I'm praying and obeying because I want to, not because I have to (Psalm 40:8).

When a whole congregation embraces this mindset, God is most surely glorified. And He does His greatest work as He promises to pour out His blessings! In John 15, Jesus warns us that apart from Him we can do nothing (self-sufficiency). But, on the other hand, when we abide in Him and are connected to Him as our source of life and purpose, we will see fruit, more fruit, much fruit (John 15:1-8).

Opportunities

God invites us to embrace our reliance upon Him through a variety of means. Obviously there are basics like Bible reading, Scripture memorization, prayer, and acts of worship and devotion. But there are other more specific things that have helped me see my continual need for Jesus, and they challenge the church as well.

Confession and the Inner Man

When I'm self-aware, I notice things going on below the surface that generally reveal a lack of trust in my life. When I notice these things rising up in me, they are an indicator that my heart is drifting and my focus is more on me than God. Here are just a few that I have to monitor:

Defensiveness	Pessimism	Sleeplessness
Disproportionate anger	Unhealthy drive	Inordinate desires
A demanding spirit	Persistent stress	Escapist thoughts

An essential step for me is to spend quality time searching my heart for these indicators and then to acknowledge my sin in an intentional, detailed, and specific way.

When I'm unaware of the deeper recesses of my life, it's easy for me to think I'm doing better than I really am. And when I think I'm doing better than I really am, it's easy to think that I don't need God as much as I really do. As Jesus taught us in the Sermon on the Mount, when I go deeper than just basic morality and behaviors, I am still a desperately sinful man who needs Christ as much today as the day I came to faith.

Therefore, I must regularly confess my inclination to control things, as well as how I can subtly manipulate circumstances, people, and even the Word of God in order to get my way or the results I desire. I must confess that much of my drive and intensity in ministry is really more about my need for validation than my passion for serving God. I must also acknowledge that I care way too much about what other people think and that I sometimes allow fear to hold me back.

Oftentimes it takes authentic conversations with fellow believers to help me uncover these blind spots. And when they are revealed, it leads to a place of brokenness and repentance, reminding me over and over again that I am insufficient and that I need God (Psalm 51).

Sabbath

I like to work. I want to work. I have more to do and more that I want to do than I can possibly get done. Yet God calls me to rest, not because I have everything done, but because He wants me to stop and take a break.

A Sabbath rest reminds us that we are not in charge. It enforces our smallness and tells us that "the Galaxy will somehow manage without me for this hour, this day, and so we are invited—nay, commanded—to relax and enjoy our relative unimportance, our humble place in a very large world."[8] The whole idea of rest exposes our temptation to be self-sufficient. When we feel the need to take every phone call, to respond to every e-mail, to meet every demand for our time, and to work around the clock, we are playing God.

When we are able to turn off and live within God-inspired boundaries, we are being dependent upon Him. We are trusting that God will give us the time, energy, and opportunity to do what needs to be done.

The Prayer List

Going through the "prayer list" at my church is a practical way to keep me reliant. There are so many needs, and it's so overwhelming to see all of them that I find myself being reminded of how small I am, how large the need is, how broken people are, and how utterly incapable we are of caring for all of them. When I'm onstage doing my thing and working within my giftedness, I'm tempted to think things are under control and that I'm doing okay. When I'm alone in the sanctuary praying for the dozens upon dozens of hurting people in my church, I am humbled and reminded that this is beyond my ability to fix.

The Undesired Gifts

There are also things that happen to us that we would rather avoid. Actually, we pray that these things don't happen. We run from them—protect ourselves from them. And, usually, we get sad or angry when they occur. Yet I can honestly say that I've come to a place in my life where I genuinely believe that they are gifts from God. They are blessings wrapped in the form of pain that help move us closer to the Lord and remind us of our insufficiency.

Illness
    Rejection
        Criticism
            Loneliness
                Failure
                    Delays
                        Migraines
                            Urgent requests
                                Relational Tension

These things drain us, distract us from our agendas, and leave us frustrated. We hate them and do everything we can to avoid them. But I'm coming to see them as opportunities—gifts that lead us to acknowledge God and our need for Him.

Steps of Faith

We are also drawn toward God when the Lord calls us to do things outside our comfort zone. When we're prompted to step into things that go beyond our understanding (Proverbs 3:5-6), our cleverness (Proverbs 23:4), and our desire for guaranteed results, we are stretched and brought to our knees with the realization that without God, there is no way it can work.

Many of us in ministry are holding back. We have dreams that are lying dormant. We have passions that we've shoved aside and talents that we've buried. The list of excuses is long and impressive. But when you get right down to it, we're scared. We don't think we can succeed. The risk of failure is too great, and because we can't manage it, control it, or be certain of success, we choose to shrink back and hide in a world where we feel safe. Rather than following our hearts and trusting God to do what only God can do, we would rather stay in the boat than join Peter on the waves.

Sometimes it takes steps of faith, undesired gifts, exposure to overwhelming need, rest, or an awareness of our sin for us to come back and acknowledge our dependency upon Jesus. What God really wants is for us to do this voluntarily and to do it regularly.

I've heard it said, "Relying on God has to begin all over again every day." It is a continual process that must occur deep within the heart. Without it, we are limiting God and all that He wants to do through us.

Corporate Seductions

Even as we look for opportunities to be reliant upon Christ, we must also be aware of the things that can distract us and pull us away. As I look at the present landscape of the church, I see three subtle enemies that can undermine leaders and their dependency upon Jesus. None of them are actually harmful in and of themselves. Yet they have the potential to be abused, over-emphasized, and implemented in such a manner that they deteriorate our trust in God and subsequently place the results of the Kingdom directly in our own hands. I refer to them as the 3M's:

Manufacturing

First of all, we love to make things happen. As a common leadership mantra goes, "If it's gonna be, it's up to me." This appeals to our flesh, especially type A personalities, and it drives us to make ministry happen with or without Jesus. Subtly, we go from being distributers of ministry to becoming manufacturers.[9] Rather than seeing ourselves as conduits through whom God is working, we internally believe that we have to drive things. It falls on us to make it happen and to gain the expected outcomes we crave. So we lean on our giftedness, our passion, and our hard work to get results for God.

Christian Schwartz refers to this as "technocratic church growth," or the belief that growth is a result of experts and skill alone.[10] With so many conferences, books, blogs, and resources, it's never been easier to believe that we can make it happen. We convince ourselves that all we need is to find the right expert, the right book, the right theory, and/or the right source of wisdom, and then, once we apply what they tell us, we'll get the results we desire. So, let's get busy and make it happen. That's manufacturing ministry.

Eugene Peterson speculates that this is the primary reason that so many in vocational ministries leave prematurely. It may also be the reason for so many moral failures. We seize hold of the assumption that if we just work hard enough or get the right information we will get the kind of results we want. When that doesn't happen, pastors give up, quit, or get fired.

Managing

Another problem is related to how we manage ministry. It is the need to plan, prepare, structure, organize, and control things. Obviously, some of this is needed, especially when a church is growing and moves beyond a single cell. At some point we need to develop processes and policies and move beyond just getting by with duct tape and flying by the seat of our pants.

Yet most of us have control issues—or at least we have board members who have control issues. As a result, we can easily estrange the Holy Spirit in favor of strategy, planning, preparation, marketing, and the like. Our competency begins to drive things more than the sovereign and mysterious power of God. Much like David trying to fight Goliath in Saul's armor, we have preconceived ideas of what and how things should be done, and then we force ministry to fit those molds. This leads to the next step, which is to put people and programs under our thumbs in order to prevent problems and keep everything in order.

On top of that, we feed this attitude and enable it to flourish in the hearts of our congregations. Consumerism has pushed many ministries to be driven by what people "want," which is usually a series of practical tools to help them better manage their lives. Generally, this is nothing more than self-help material with a few Bible verses tacked on the end as proof texts. I'm not opposed to helping people, but too often we start with our plans and agendas and then go to the Bible for support. Rather than allowing God to take the lead, we use Him as a spare tire while we take the wheel.

In his challenging book *Real Church*, Larry Crabb says it this way: "Unbroken people set our sights on what we can manage. With the right talent and enough charisma, any gathering can stir people's emotions, create the illusion of transcendence, generate and experience what we'd swear was worship, and help us feel better. Add in practical instruction for managing negative emotions and doable strategies for communicating more effectively as spouses, parents, friends and colleagues, and people will not only feel better, we'll live better. We'll live happier, more successful lives, without really needing God, certainly not the cross of Christ or the power of His Spirit."[11]

Measuring

Finally, there is our need to measure things into tangible outcomes. Some of this is healthy and needed. There is a book in the Bible called Numbers, and we read about all kinds of specifics in the book of Acts. Jesus told us that we will know a tree by its fruit. So, on the positive side, we need to evaluate and not be afraid of facts, numbers, dashboards, and metrics. There is great value in these tools, and they help us "define reality," which healthy organizations do.

Further, we often get what we measure, and if we aren't measuring anything, we usually lack focus and don't see tangible results, especially in larger ministries that are moving fast. I get that. Yet too often we attempt to reduce the definition of success in ministry to only measurable outcomes. When that happens, we are entering into dangerous territory.

For example, we try to measure things we have no business measuring. Recently I opened a book from a source I respect greatly, but when I read the first chapter and saw that they were trying to convince me that we could develop tools to measure the condition of a person's heart, I couldn't believe what I was reading. I agree that our actions do reflect our hearts, but to suggest that we can *effectively* measure the maturity and condition of someone's inner being is both foolish and arrogant.

Once we go down this path, we can find that we're tempted to focus only on the things we can measure and to manipulate things in order to get the desired results. Acts of grace and love can get minimized in favor of more glamorous events, like mass conversions. I am a bit skeptical when I read about a church having 832 conversions simply because people were asked to raise their hands in a service. That is a bunch of "dung" (to use biblical language). In many cases we have reduced conversion to a prayer and a raised hand so that we can tweet about it and pat ourselves on the back. Deep down, we know that 832 people were not truly converted. Unfortunately, it's not uncommon to see churches boast about "hundreds" of conversions each year and yet have no overall growth in attendance. It's a revolving door of watered-down decisions.

On the other hand, how do we measure comforting a widow after the death of a spouse? Do we tell her to read a book? Do we shove her off on a counselor, support group, or small group so we can say we've done our job? Does it take one visit? Three? Five? What I've found is that people are different, and different widows have different needs. But if I'm trying to measure everything, I'm tempted to herd this person into a process without really knowing her as a person, without loving her, getting into her soul, discerning what she needs and where God is in her grief. Like Job's comforters, I just want to give her a trite solution, feel like I did my job, and then move on to more important things, rather than just sit with her in her pain.

Once again, I'm not suggesting that measuring things is always bad or inappropriate. I don't want to throw the proverbial baby out with the bath water. The 3M's have value, and some churches need to lean into them. Yet I feel that, in general, we have placed an unhealthy emphasis upon them, and we have been seduced into controlling and driving ministry on our terms more than trusting in God. As a result, many of us are bearing more stress, more pressure, and more weight than God expects us to carry. Others are falsely assuming God is at work in their ministry more than He may be.

Another way to say it is this: we are sinning.

Much like King David, we feel more comfortable taking a census and numbering our troops rather than walking in faith and reliance upon God (1 Chronicles 21). This allows us to be in control and enables us to discern how we can make things happen by implementing the 3M's. This is a safer path, a more predictable path. But we forget that God rebuked David because his actions were sinful and reflected a lack of faith.

In the classic booklet *Tyranny of the Urgent*, Charles Hummel writes, "The root of all sin is self-sufficiency—independence from God. When we fail to wait prayerfully for God's guidance and strength, we are saying, with our actions if not our lips, that we do not need him."[12] When we are self-sufficient, we are in essence proclaiming to the Lord that we can do ministry without Him. We are marginalizing God, throwing our elbows out, and indulging our flesh, whether we mean to or not. As a result, we stand convicted by the words attributed to St. Augustine, "What could be greedier than a man for whom God is not enough?"

On the other hand, by making genuine dependence an *Activator* that we cultivate into our lives and the lives of our congregations, we are fighting against our fleshly bent. We are honoring God, and we are walking in reliance and faith. As a result, the culture of the church is made healthier, and a context is created where God's Word and the Spirit are able to more effectively bear fruit through us.

Chapter 6

TEACHABLE SPIRIT

"It's what you learn after you know it all that counts." — *John Wooden*

In the movie *Thor*, the young, arrogant warrior disregards the wisdom of his father and the promptings of his closest friends. He recklessly charges ahead, picking fights and believing he knows best in all situations. Eventually, consequences happen, and he is banished from his home of Asgard and sent to Earth without the use of his powerful hammer. After a period of time, Thor finds himself at rock bottom and meekly acknowledges, "I have much to learn. I know that now." It is only then that things begin to turn for Thor. When his heart softens, he once again finds life, power, and purpose.

People with teachable spirits realize the value of humility and how little they actually know before consequences force them to act. They accept the fact they are not as smart, competent, or knowledgeable as they are tempted to believe. They are willing to seek out new insights, information, perspectives, and applications. They seek wisdom and are willing to wrestle with and entertain new ideas, new practices, and new processes. They are open to God's Spirit and leading. They hold to their convictions with grace and humility.

When a congregation is filled with such people, the soil is enriched.

Hopeless

George Barna's book *Turnaround Churches* is based on principles that were gleaned from several struggling churches which were able to successfully transition and experience significant renewal. While this book is very helpful, there is one thing about it that troubles me. Barna does say that "openness of the people" is a given.[13] In other words, all the characteristics and principles he shares are basically useless if the people are not receptive to leadership or to new ways of approaching ministry. Without a teachable spirit, the potential to turn around a struggling church is rather hopeless, in his opinion. However, Barna gives no suggestions about how to foster the "openness of the people" that he advocates.

Without members who have teachable spirits, a church becomes rigid, inflexible, and resistant to practical and spiritual insights that God may use to enhance their effectiveness. They will almost always gravitate to living in the past, choosing predictability over opening themselves up to the possibility that God may be doing a new thing. They tend to turn inward, closing themselves off from anything outside their own experience and comfort. And when a church is closed-off… it's a turn-off. When the church is unteachable… it's unreachable.

This takes us back to the premise of this book: dirt matters. Bad soil, the worst soil, is packed down, hardened, and unreceptive. Nothing grows. That's what happens with an unteachable spirit.

Reversing It

Knowing that teachability is a key element for a healthy church culture, the thought comes to mind, *Can a church that is not teachable change? Is it really possible for people who think they have all the answers to suddenly open up and become receptive?* While it's very hard, the answer is a resounding yes.

When God spoke to Manasseh, one of the most depraved and arrogant kings of Judah, he and the people of Israel "paid no attention." But God was able to eventually get his attention, and then "in his distress he sought the favor of the Lord his God and humbled himself greatly before the Lord" (2 Chronicles

33:10-12). Manasseh suddenly began to listen, learn, and change his ways.
Once he did, the nation followed suit.

What happened to Manasseh can still happen today.

A pastor with whom I worked was leading a small and slowly growing church.
His board members were resistant, cautious, and hesitant at almost every turn.
They laughed at, criticized, and outright rejected many of his ideas without
much discussion. Even when they accepted new things initially, once someone
in the church complained, the leaders would retreat. On multiple occasions,
the pastor thought about leaving because he was weary and convinced the
church board would never come around. One day he called me and said that
something amazing had happened. The board had called him in, apologized,
expressed openness, and said they wanted to change.

Even when individuals, boards, or congregations as a whole seem to be
unteachable, change is possible. The tide can be reversed, and openness can
happen.

Becoming Aware

Perhaps the biggest obstacle we face in this area is that almost all of us see
ourselves as being teachable. In other words, having a closed spirit and a hard
heart isn't really a problem for us. We actually see ourselves as being very open
to instruction when, in reality, we may not be.

Several years ago I was asked to meet with a church board in another town.
They were trying to implement small groups and were failing miserably.
Shortly after our meeting began, I could see at least part of their problem.

This church had a Sunday school program, Sunday morning worship services,
a Sunday evening service, and a Wednesday night all-church Bible Study.
Then they added small groups on top of all these other programs. I told
them that part of their problem was they were offering too much and had
unrealistic expectations if they thought a majority of families were going to
attend all these functions, serve in ministry, and participate in a small group.
That was a minimum of six weekly commitments they were expecting people

to make. In addition, they were expecting people to process and apply an unrealistic amount of new information by having that many different lessons each week.

As I was sharing this, the lead elder snapped back, "I don't agree with that." For the next several minutes, I inquired about why he disagreed, and I tried to explain small groups cannot be effective if they are just another program tacked on to an already busy calendar of events. This elder would not budge. He insisted my insight had no merit and was convinced that the solution had to do with curriculum, scheduling, or something else. I'm quite sure that in his own eyes, he saw himself as being very teachable because he was looking for a solution. But from my perspective, he was inflexible, stubborn, and closed-off.

A similar situation occurred when a member of my church came into my office upset. She was studying the Bible daily, reading books, and downloading sermons on the Second Coming. She couldn't understand why I was not focusing more attention on that issue, rather than the series I was currently doing on relationships. Knowing that this woman refused to share the same bed with her husband, didn't want to go to counseling, was telling people she hated her mate, and was engaged in an emotionally inappropriate relationship with someone else, I asked, "Is it possible that your studying of the Second Coming is a way to escape the more significant heart issues in your life?" Then I added, "If you would like, I am willing to do an expository study with you on Ephesians 5 or 1 Corinthians 7. That would give you a chance to dig deeper into God's Word and address the most relevant issue in your life at the same time." This person left and started to attend a new church where she could study the Bible and continue to compartmentalize her heart, never dealing with the deeper areas of sin in her life. She saw herself as being very teachable, yet in reality her heart was hard, closed, and bitter.

But the problem is not just with others—it's with us. Actually, it's with me.

After my first draft of this chapter, one of my editors told me that my tone was a bit condescending and that it appeared I was grinding my axe at points. As I re-read my work, I began to see how I was writing from a place of judgment. I was venting my frustration with a subset of Christendom that upsets me because of the arrogance and harshness I perceive in them as they defend the truth. As a result, I've had to rewrite this chapter multiple times, and I fear I still haven't gotten it right. The reason is that my heart is prone to pride. It's easy to perceive a lack of teachability in others and miss it in myself.

Just as the Pharisees were blind to their blindness, we, too, can be sincere and passionate and yet still resistant to what God is trying to say to us. For many years when I read the gospels, I envisioned myself standing behind Jesus as He called out the Pharisees. Now, I realize I've got more in common with them than I would like to admit. Failure to see my own depravity and a tendency to assume I'm always in the right leads me to the same self-righteous, arrogant, and closed-off narrow-mindedness that caused the Pharisees to miss Jesus. It's always harder to hear what God is saying when we assume that we've already got it figured out. And more often than I would like to admit, I think I have it figured out.

As dangerous as this is for the individual believer, it is even more toxic for a church body. When an overall mindset that they have arrived settles into a congregation, it breeds arrogance, judgment, and an unteachable spirit. This pollutes the soil and limits what God can do in and through that church body.

Specific Barricades

There are several ways an unteachable spirit can sneak in and manifest itself. Each of these enables individual believers or a congregation as a whole to turn inward and harden themselves to things God may want to reveal. None of us are immune to these instinctive yet damaging barricades to our maturation.

Labeling

This is the temptation to make snap judgments or act on assumptions and then, based on that, to force people into categories that allow us to write off anything they say. We use terms like liberal, fundamentalist, reformed, prosperity gospel, emerging, or heretic. Each of these conjures up images in our minds and leads us to conclusions that are either positive or negative. Sometimes these terms are necessary and true. But they also present risk. On the negative side, when we label people, we are able to place them in boxes, de-personalize them, and reject them and anything they might say. Labeling gives us an excuse not to wrestle with, think about, or evaluate the words of another. It leads to a "defend and attack" mentality and puts us into a position of power rather than humility, grace, and openness.

Cognitive Closure

People like to have a sense of control, and they hate the feeling that comes with uncertainty. Living in a fast-paced world that is constantly in flux only accelerates this inner battle. Therefore, our flesh craves what psychologists call "cognitive closure," the need to have clear and firm answers that alleviate confusion or doubt. This is understandable because people cannot remain in tension indefinitely. They need some closure to function. Yet if we're not careful, we can be so driven to seek cognitive closure that we cling to beliefs even if they are clearly unhealthy or untrue. The security that comes with having an answer leads to the impulse to grab hold of a belief and then close the door, thereby eliminating worry and providing us with security. Anything that challenges that belief is quickly avoided and rejected because we fear ambiguity.

The Living and the Dead

Have you ever noticed that Christians tend to be more open to the writings of someone outside of their tradition after that author is dead? When people are no longer living, we feel more comfortable wading through their material, and we are usually more patient with potentially damaging statements or beliefs.[14] We can qualify statements, pick and choose, and write off what we reject. When we encounter living people with views outside our comfort zones, we tend be very cautious and critical, often assuming the worst and jumping to conclusions. Therefore, we reject fresh insights and new thoughts until the author dies, and then we tend to become more open to wrestling with his or her material.

Celibacy of the Intellect

Warren Bennis coined the phrase "celibacy of the intellect" to describe leaders who are hesitant to reflect upon whether their actions, decisions, and behaviors are proper and effective. He observed that too many people charge ahead without considering what they are doing, how they are doing it, or whether it is truly effective. Busyness, insecurity, and the shame associated with failure make it difficult for us to slow down and honestly evaluate if our beliefs, values, and actions are on-target. It's much easier to keep pressing ahead and then blame other people or circumstances when things don't go as planned.

The Vacuum

We live in the information age, and as a result, we are tempted to equate spiritual knowledge with books, blogs, sermons, conferences, etc. Yet our greatest lessons often come out of experience, observation, reflection, and listening. I am convinced that our greatest spiritual growth occurs in the context of relationships. It's sitting down with people and talking about the heart, about life, and about God and His Word. When we make an idol out of information, we learn in a contextual vacuum, and we can easily filter information, spin it, and manipulate it to our benefit. Without objective people to push, question, challenge, and help us process what we're learning, we are likely not learning as much as we think. Rather, we are simply controlling the information and taking comfort in a false security that we're "going deeper."

The God App

Many of us have a hard time with mystery and process. We want a system that gives answers, preferably airtight ones. Therefore, rather than wrestling with God when facing theological and ethical dilemmas, we seek the fastest, easiest answers available and settle for simple and trite solutions to issues that are often complex. No need to embrace a process that may not yield an answer— just download an app or Google it. Any answer beats nothing—except when God doesn't give us an answer because He's trying to teach us something far bigger and richer about Himself than the issue we're trying to figure out.

Guilt by Association

It amazes me how we are able to rationalize and disregard what Jesus taught about judging others. There are few more shallow and elementary ways that we do this than when we play the "guilt by association" game. If I talk with, read, hang out with, or quote another person, then it is assumed I am endorsing her ideology and all her beliefs. Like modern politicians, we've become so proficient at this that most people are scared to engage anyone outside of their acceptable circle out of fear that they will be labeled and judged. This keeps us isolated and insulated.

Through My Eyes Only

One of the positive results of postmodern thinking is that history and truth are no longer just assumed. Now, the sources and perspectives of stories are examined under a hermeneutic of suspicion. Sometimes this can get out of control, but at other times it's priceless. Try reading or watching *Flags of Our Fathers* and *Letters from Iwo Jima* back to back. It's a sobering experience to reflect on that battle, not just through the eyes of America, but also through the perspective of Japanese soldiers. Occasionally we need to step outside of ourselves in order to see and evaluate things through someone else's eyes. This is most effective when we read biographies or build relationships with people who hold different worldviews or come from culturally different backgrounds than we do. But this can get messy and uncomfortable, and it can expose how we are sheltered from and ignorant of the experiences and insights of others. Therefore, it's very tempting to just avoid the discomfort of a new perspective and trust that our understanding is universal.

Group Think

Sometimes what we call learning is really nothing more than regurgitated teaching and intellectual fluff that serves little purpose besides reiterating what we already believe. I know someone who attends a church where the pastor uses commentaries from a nationally known preacher and encourages the church to use this same person's study Bible. Whenever this author's latest book comes out, everyone at the church is giddy with anticipation. Most of the adult Sunday school classes use this same person's curriculum as well. When cults do this, we call it dangerous and brainwashing. When Protestants do it, we call it discipleship and going deeper. We all have our favorite authors, preachers, and teachers, but there's a big world out there where God is using a lot of people to convey His message.

Fixing

Eugene Peterson rightly notes: "I think pastors are the worst listeners. We're so used to speaking, teaching, giving answers. We must learn to be quiet, quit being so verbal, learn to pay attention to what's going on, and listen. It's not only about listening to the Bible, it's about listening to people—taking time to hear the nuances in their voices and language, and repeat what we're hearing. We're all very poorly educated in this business."[15] When we get caught up in the role of always trying to fix everyone else, we don't have time to reflect on what might be broken in our own lives or what we might learn from the person we're trying to help. Like the guy who recently cornered me at church and talked non-stop about how much God was teaching him to be quiet and listen, we can easily become so focused on helping everyone else that we are not helping ourselves. This leads to an infatuation with what others need, so even when we are learning something, it becomes more about sharing it with others than it does about internalizing and applying it ourselves.

These ten barricades are real, and they can naturally manifest themselves without warning. But ultimately they are damaging, often fostering pride and making the soil of our hearts hard and, therefore, less productive.

Nurturing Teachability

In order to establish teachability in the life of the church, there are several things that can be done. Here are just a few:

Define Your Core Convictions

One thing that scares people is the notion that if they open themselves up to one thing, they will have to open themselves up to all things. If they change their opinion or belief in one area, then they will be required to do so in all areas. As irrational as this may sound, it is often real, and when it hits people, they are paralyzed with fear. One way to handle it is to give them the confidence of knowing some things will remain stable.

I have found addressing the difference between essentials and non-essentials in doctrine helps, as does illustrating and pointing out the difference between truth and traditions when it comes to methodology. Essentials and truth are constant; they will not be compromised. But non-essentials and traditions can and should be evaluated. By highlighting the items that will remain fixed, people often can relax and take on a less guarded posture with secondary items.

A friend of mine has found when he and his wife are having problems in their marriage, it helps them to purposely tell each other, "I'm here, and I'm not going anywhere." My friend tells me that this provides a sense of security and reminds them their core fear of being rejected and having the relationship fall apart is not going to happen. This affirmation gives them confidence to wrestle with the issue at hand without allowing irrational fears to take over. In much the same way, when we solidify our core convictions to the church, it gives people confidence to wrestle with issues without succumbing to the fear of heresy or the fear that everything is going to fall apart.

Instruct Proactively

We must teach on teachability.

We can teach the "love principle" and the emphasis in the New Testament on relationships. Agape is the premier sign of maturity, and "knowledge puffs up, but love builds up" (1 Corinthians 8:1). Information alone can be mastered and feeds our pride, but relationships can never be mastered, and, therefore, they keep us humble and constantly expose our sinfulness.

We can teach on the importance of having a childlike faith. Jesus used children as the ideal example, even when His disciples tried to dismiss them. Most children possess humility, wonder, trust, and openness. Many adults tend to struggle with these.

We can teach on the book of Proverbs, which emphasizes the importance of gaining wisdom, obtaining knowledge, listening to others, and being humble, while also addressing the consequences of being stubborn.

We can teach on the Pharisees, digging into their origins, practices, and extreme devotion to the Torah. Teaching from an expository and historical perspective on this issue, we can illustrate how easy it is to become a Pharisee without even knowing it and the consequences that result from this.[16]

We can teach on Job's comforters and how people feel the need to explain problems, sufferings, and challenges even when there is no explanation. Job's comforters show how shallow and pathetic it is when we try to ascribe dogmatic answers to questions that God has left obscure.

We can teach on the kings of Israel and the people's response to the Old Testament prophets.

The main thing is that we proactively and consistently teach people in ways that instruct, model, and illustrate the importance of being open to practical and spiritual truth.

Exposure to Other Circles

When I was in seminary, I was required to do a research paper on someone outside of my tradition. I chose the Black Liberation theologian James Cone. When I first began to read Professor Cone's writing, I found myself getting frustrated and even angry. Yet as I read more, reflected, and processed, at some point the light went on. I began to get a glimpse of the New Testament through the experience of minorities.

When Dr. Cone stated that Jesus was black, I began to see what he was saying and the point he was making. Namely, he meant that Jesus identifies with the plight of the marginalized, the alienated, and the poor more than those in power. Since Jesus fully understands the minority experience, it can be said that He is black.

That's not to say that I agreed with all of his conclusions because I didn't. But reading Cone's work opened my eyes and gave me a greater awareness of assumptions and biases that I had previously not seen in my white, western, Protestant theology. It helped me read the New Testament from another perspective, and I found multiple verses popping off the page with fresh meaning.

Sometimes we need to push people to experience material that is beyond their normal sphere of exposure. Take them to a conference. Invite a special speaker, such as a missionary from another land. Ask the congregation to read a book. Don't do it in vacuum—do it in community, allowing for debate and even disagreement.

I was recently reading about a one-day conference sponsored by Dr. James MacDonald called "The Elephant Room." The purpose is to gather a small number of church leaders with differing opinions, practices, and beliefs for the purpose of gracious dialogue. This isn't a feel-good experience where egos are stroked and participants are told that they're equally right. It has heated moments and firm debate. I think it's awesome! But it amazes me how many people are threatened by this and even angry that Dr. MacDonald would offer such a forum. For them, it's too much to have honest dialogue or even to attempt to listen to someone with a different opinion.

We need to encourage people to occasionally read outside their normal circles of influence, not just for the purposes of critiquing, head-hunting, and playing the role of truth police, but also to be edified, challenged, and forced to think. In doing so, we do not abandon our responsibility to protect our congregations and guard against false doctrine. Nor do we overwhelm them or encourage them to take everything hook, line, and sinker.

We simply need to realize that God may, in fact, be speaking in and through people with whom we disagree (Philippians 1:15-18). I understand this is harder for those who genuinely believe they have a corner on the truth. But a casual look at history will show an avalanche of people who thought they were in the right, only to find, in time, that they were in the wrong. If the Kingdom of God belongs to a child, then perhaps God may be able to teach us something, even from those with whom we disagree or whom we consider less mature.

Reflect It

Leaders must model a teachable spirit in tangible ways. If we are not teaching new things or illustrating from our own life stories, failures, lessons learned, or new challenges that we are struggling with, our people won't be teachable either. Have we ever publicly shared a story illustrating when we made a mistake, stumbled in sin, or were wrong on something? Have we ever apologized?

I talked to a man who had lost his business and his family as a result of his drinking problem. It was through a 12-step program that he was able to break free and eventually come to Christ. He then got involved in a church where his faith began to grow. But from day one he noticed a key difference between the people in the 12-step program and the Christians he was meeting at church. That difference was honesty about their struggles, temptations, and sins. Over time that difference became even more concrete. This man confessed with great passion how much he believed in the truth of the gospel yet how frustrated he was at the lack of transparency he saw among Christians. He lamented the fact that there was peer pressure at church to "have it together," and that only his AA meetings provided a place where he could drop his guard and be real.

We have to move beyond information, stale sermons, and surface-level Christianity. If we cannot get real and be transparent with our people, our people are not going to get real in return. I understand that some people aren't ready to handle transparency, so we need to have discernment about how far to push and when to push. But we must push. We must move beyond the safe and superficial elements of our faith, modeling honesty and teachability as godly and biblical traits.

Pray for Consequence

If all else fails, we need to have the courage to ask God to shake us up. Sometimes that's what it takes. God needs to rock our world. Just as people who have near-death experiences tend to return with a different posture and a new attitude toward life, sometimes God just needs to break us. He has to humble us in order to help us see how little we know and how much there is to learn.

That's what it took for Thor. That's what it took for Manasseh. And that's what it often took for the Israelites: "Whenever God slew them, they would seek Him; they would eagerly turn to Him again" (Psalm 78:34).

Humility leads to teachability.

We can either choose to embrace humility and a teachable spirit, or we can wait for God to drop circumstances into our lives that force our hands. When hearts are hard and the ground needs to be softened, we might need to pray for God to get our attention—to do something which forces us to the end of ourselves—because when we are humbled, we are often most receptive to what God is doing and saying.

It's no accident that the Latin word for ground or soil, *humus*, is also the root of the English word humility. When people stand firm on their convictions and yet have a humble and teachable spirit, this humility nurtures an environment in which God does His best work. Being teachable does carry risk, but the reward of nurturing good soil far outweighs the self-imposed limitation of a proud, callused, and closed-off heart.

Chapter 7

SUSTAINABLE IMPACT

*"Idealism: The tendency to represent things in their
ideal forms, rather than as they are."*

I know of a church that is on their fourth or fifth pastor in the past fifteen years. Attendance grew under every one of the previous ministers, yet the church is still the same size they were fifteen years ago. This may sound like a riddle, but it's a true story. Let me explain why.

This congregation has a core of around 75 people. They want the church to reach others and make an impact for Christ. So, they seek out a pastor who shares that vision and has the giftedness to go along with it. The church begins to attract new people who come to faith and start attending regularly. There is an increase in attendance. On at least one occasion, the church had more than doubled in size, and the leadership was talking about building an addition.

In each case, the people were excited. Early on, they were positive, energized, and enthusiastic. Then, at some point, usually a couple of years into the tenure of the senior pastor, the core members would suddenly start to get nervous. The board would become more conservative and resistant, pushing back on the minister, expressing concerns over smaller issues and discouraging anything new.

Eventually a "we/they" mentality would begin to settle in, and while the people were civil and externally polite, the core group would start to turn inward, causing the new folks to feel marginalized. The board would then become heavy-handed, and eventually, the minister would resign out of exasperation or be fired for some illegitimate reason. Most of the new people would leave, and the church would return to the size it was before.

Then the pattern would repeat itself again. The details would change, but the storyline was the same.

I have talked with two of the former pastors of this church. Each one has said basically the same thing, "I just don't get it. Things were going so well. The church had so much potential. And for no reason the attitude of the board and the core group began to change. It's just so disappointing."

Almost every congregation wants to be used by God. The problem is we usually have an idealistic view of what that means. We glamorize ministry, and outreach specifically, wanting to believe that it's going to occur naturally or that it will be fun, easy, and smooth.

We have stars in our eyes.

As a result, when reality hits and things get difficult, some churches are unwilling to do what is necessary to make sustained impact possible. Even if they are fortunate enough to see growth occurring, they get squirrelly and sabotage themselves once they are outside their comfort zone.

This dynamic of idealism is not just about attractional church models. Even missional churches that couldn't care less about how many people come to their gathering will see consequences once their actions start bearing fruit and the size and personality of their core begin to change.

For an existing church to reach their redemptive potential, they must desire to make a difference for the Kingdom, and they must embrace a realistic view of what that means, understanding that reaching people and expanding their influence comes at a cost. Even if they know it's going to be hard, it's much harder than they realize.

Ok with Messy

Whenever a church gets new people and starts new ministries, new problems arise. More people and more programs mean even more problems. As a result, things get messy.

In the book of Acts, we read how the church was impacting people and was growing rapidly as a result. The disciples were facing persecution outside the church, but inside, things were wonderful. People were coming to Christ. Worship, miracles, and a tremendous sense of unity characterized the faith community. Benevolence was winning the day; people were being cared for, and needs were being met. They were turning the world upside down, and the future was bright. But then something happened.

> *"In those days when the number of disciples was increasing, the Hellenistic Jews among them complained against the Hebraic Jews because their widows were being overlooked in the daily distribution of food."* Acts 6:1 (NIV)

Suddenly, there is an internal problem. Division and complaining have begun, and at the heart of it is racial tension. It is threatening to divide the church. When the church in Jerusalem was smaller, this wasn't an issue. But now that it's growing, it is.

new people = new problems
more people = more problems

Different People

Even today, most everyone likes the idea of impacting a growing number of lives—until people start showing up who don't look like them or act like them. It's all good until they find themselves sitting next to someone who doesn't use deodorant. Or "that family," the one with kids who run wild in the hallways, starts coming every week. Or they suddenly find out that a new, unsanctioned small group has started outside the main entrance and their primary activity is smoking and throwing the butts on the ground. Or people start coming who don't have anything to give, but have a long list of needs.

If you are reaching people and your fellowship is growing, and especially if you live in an urban context, it only gets more interesting. You may get teenagers who show up dressed in Goth clothing. A girl who works at the nightclub may turn up on Sunday with a thong showing. A gay couple may decide to visit and sit through the service holding hands. Or you may have an unmarried couple who is living together sign up to lead a small group.

How do I know these things? We've experienced them all. And then some.

Back when the disciples were in the upper room praying, they didn't have to worry about foreigners and Gentiles. They were a fairly homogenous group of Jewish believers who had all been part of Jesus' inner circle. But once the church started growing, a number of Gentiles and Hellenistic Jews were converting and relocating in Jerusalem.

This led to silos. Camps. Division. Racial Tension. Things were getting messy.

Different Languages

It wasn't just that there were different people coming into the church at Jerusalem, but the heart of the problem was the fact that they didn't speak the same language. The Hellenistic Jews did not speak Hebrew, or at least not enough to communicate their needs. Therefore, they were left out. Neglected. Marginalized.

The verb tense for "being overlooked" indicates that this was not a one-time problem but one that was continually happening. Hebraic Jews either were too preoccupied to notice, or they flat out didn't care that foreign widows were being neglected. After all, they probably had an attitude that if those people are going to be in our town, they need to speak our language.

Some time back, my six-year-old son was in the garage, and I came up behind him and said his name. It startled him. He jumped, turned, and said to me, "Dude, that's not cool." I laughed and gave him a hug. He was speaking the language of his generation. But when I walked away, I thought to myself, *What would have happened if I would have called my dad "dude"?* I think he would have just stared at me, shook his head, and asked me if I was on drugs.

Then I thought about what might have happened if my dad had called his dad "dude"? I think he might have gotten thumped for being disrespectful. But my son wasn't being impolite, and he wasn't on drugs; he was simply speaking a new language. It was the language of his generation.

I remember the first time we had a worship leader onstage wearing sandals and jeans with holes in them. And the time we had someone serve communion in shorts. Then there was the young believer who sat through worship with a hat on. And people carrying coffee cups into the sanctuary. In each situation, some of our members were gravely concerned that these people were being disrespectful and that they were hurting the testimony of the church. That was not the case—they were just speaking a different language. In each situation, their hearts did not mean to disrespect anyone; they were just being themselves and didn't know any better.

Church members generally love the idea of impact because they want to believe the church is going to influence people like them and that there will be natural connections. But if the church impacts people and grows—really grows—and especially if it attracts people far from God, it's likely to attract some people who are not like them. And when you have more people, new people, and different people, things get uncomfortable.

Evolution

Another kind of messiness happens when a church is having impact. The systems, structures, and processes of ministry evolve and change. Too often, churches think they can reach and assimilate more people without a lot of change. They believe that if they just tweak a few things, people will come, and things will continue the way they always have, only with more people present. But this is a bad assumption. When people are being impacted and growth occurs, almost everything changes, just as it did in Acts 6.

> *"So the Twelve gathered all the disciples together and said, 'It would not be right for us to neglect the ministry of the word of God in order to wait on tables. Brothers and sisters, choose seven men from among you who are known to be full of the Spirit and wisdom. We will turn this responsibility over to them and*

will give our attention to prayer and the ministry of the word.'"
Acts 6:2-4 (NIV)

There is little doubt that the quickest and easiest solution for the problem in Jerusalem was for the disciples to take care of the issue by serving the food. But they refused and said they had to focus on other things. Their response implies that some, if not most, of the people expected them to step in and take care of it personally. But they didn't.

The solution the disciples proposed for delegating the responsibility of serving food makes sense to us because we assume that serving food back then was the same as serving food today. It can seem like a no-brainer because anyone can pass out food and clean up tables. But there is a historical nuance to this story that makes their solution rather radical.

It was customary for the leaders to collect money and food for benevolence and then to oversee the distribution. Trusted leaders were expected to handle the money and resources. On top of that, the head of the house or the most influential person in the room was the one responsible for serving the food. Think about Jesus at the Last Supper. He was the one who broke the bread and dispersed it. He took the cup and passed it around.

The solution proposed by the disciples was radical, and it went against religious tradition and cultural expectations. But, because the disciples understood the priesthood of believers and had other responsibilities they had to focus on, they implemented a new and unorthodox process.

When a congregation grows, it requires the church to come up with new ideas, new solutions, new processes, new roles, and new expectations. This means structures change. Policies change. The budgeting process and the financial management of the church change. Communication changes, and staffing responsibilities change. There is increased complexity and a greater sense of discontinuity now that more people are involved.

The temptation is to assume what we are doing and how we are doing it will continue to work. But that doesn't scale or equate to reality. It caps out, and at some point, it no longer works. The old, proven, and safe will stop being effective. The most comfortable and easiest solutions are no longer valid.

An impacting church that is expanding service and reaching more people must think differently and act differently. Its leaders may have to make some decisions that break tradition and expectations.

There is another aspect of this that I need to address. Most churches severely underestimate the relational cost of reaching new people. They fail to understand that relational patterns will change drastically. There can be a severe loss of intimacy and increased anonymity. It's guaranteed if the church sees an influx of new converts.

The relationship church members have with the senior pastor will also change because he now has more people to serve and more responsibilities, and that means he is not as accessible as he once was. Members will hear about conversion stories but won't know the people involved, which can make them feel disconnected and out of the loop.

Relationships between members will change as well. Longtime friends may not see each other for weeks or months at a time because they are going to different services. Or a longtime member may walk up to someone and ask her if she is a visitor, only to hear her reply, "No, I've been coming for nine months." The longtime member will apologize, feel embarrassed, and likely think, *It wasn't like this before.*

All of these things and countless more unearth emotions inside of existing members. This is especially true when a congregation doubles in size.[17] Almost everything will change, and this will stir emotions in people that they don't know how to articulate, so they'll grasp for control, complain about things that aren't really important, push to turn the clock back, or even leave the church, taking others with them.

Willing to Risk

On top of things being messy and in flux, sustained impact requires risk. You can't always play it safe. Sometimes you have to strategically and intentionally step out and do things that are not guaranteed to succeed.

The solution to the growing congregation in Jerusalem required the apostles to empower seven new leaders with positions of responsibility and leadership (Acts 6:5-6). The apostles had to relinquish control and turn responsibility over to people they likely didn't know, or at least didn't know well. All seven of these men had Greek names. They were likely foreigners who had not been raised in Jerusalem, and at least one had been a Gentile convert. The apostles were giving these men authority, putting them over a ministry, and allowing them to handle money.

For a church to have impact, it *must* diffuse ministry and turn people loose. This requires risk. You have to trust people. At some point, every growing church has to address the question, "Are we most concerned with safety and control, or are we going to take the risk and release people for ministry?"

The apostles were not flippant about commissioning these men. They specifically asked for men "full of the Spirit and wisdom." Yet it doesn't change the fact that they commissioned seven people they didn't appear to know well and gave them high-level responsibility. And this wasn't an anomaly. Read the book of Acts, and you'll find that as the church exploded, things were happening on the fringes that the apostles in Jerusalem knew little or nothing about until months after those events occurred.

Look at every epistle in the New Testament, and you'll find struggles with moral, relational, and doctrinal issues. Read the gospels, and tell me if you would have given the disciples "authority" and sent them out at the same point in their training Jesus did. We are far too cautious and often fearful someone is going to make a mistake by saying something or doing something we wouldn't. Therefore, many leaders tighten up, only empowering people they deem safe, while limiting the rest.

It's risky when you release people you don't know. Once we allowed someone to come in and do special music at the suggestion of a church member. We just trusted his judgment and assumed it would be okay. The guest musician got up and sang "Let It Be" by the Beatles but didn't change the lyrics. When the singer got to the line, "Mother Mary comes to me speaking words of wisdom," I looked over at Jim Thompson, one of our elders, and I thought his head was going to explode. Fortunately, Jim handled it well. We debriefed, learned a lesson, set up a policy for special music, and moved on.

A congregation with a vision for impact and the expectation of reaching people must empower its members for ministry on the edges. If they do, they will encounter risk, and there will be mistakes, just as there were in every New Testament church. On the other hand, there is the potential to find diamonds in the rough and to see God working through people in ways you never dreamt.

Human and Divine Partnership

The story in Acts 6 ends with three phrases that highlight the incredible impact the church was having. The Word of God was spreading; the church in Jerusalem was experiencing rapid growth, and priests were coming to the faith (Acts 6:7). The first-century Jewish historian Josephus wrote that there were four tribes of priests, each with about 5,000 in number, making for roughly 20,000 Jewish priests in Jerusalem.[18] Acts tells us that a large number of them converted to Christianity!

Because the apostles were able to navigate the problem of division and neglect among the believers in Jerusalem, the church exploded with exponential growth. Yet if we are not careful, we can make a false assumption. Namely, "If we just do the right stuff, the church will automatically have impact." But is this really the case?

Brandon O'Brien, author of the book *Strategically Small Churches*, told me he did a study on each of the growth passages in the book of Acts. He found that in every case where the church grew in numbers, the growth came after some problem or challenge had been overcome. Acts 6 highlights an internal problem, and as the church dealt with that problem, God blessed them with another wave of growth. This story perfectly illustrates how a congregation's impact is directly contingent on a partnership between human responsibility and divine involvement.

God Dictates It

God is the one who gives growth (1 Corinthians 3:6-7). As a result, sometimes He blesses certain people, churches, or movements, allowing them to bear much fruit. Yet at other times, God calls people to faithful service without seeing short-term, immediate results. Look at Noah, Isaiah, and Jeremiah, for example. They preached, but no one responded positively. There was nothing to put in the newsletter except stories of rejection and failure. Even Jesus gave a hard teaching on one occasion, and many of His disciples turned back (John 6:66).

There are some congregations who find themselves in contexts where visible impact is challenging and does not come easily. My friend Rob is planting churches in the rural areas of Utah, working with Mormons. He is having an impact, but it's not likely he's going to build a megachurch with thousands of attendees. A young lady I know is working a secular job in an Islamic country but, in reality, is a missionary to that land. She is wise and patient, reflecting the love of Christ and seeing fruit, but it's not measured in mass conversions or a packed sanctuary.

Other churches have moved away from an attractional/seeker model. Their congregations have shrunk in attendance, but the leadership has never been more confident that they are in the center of God's will.[19] Don't get me wrong, they are still leading people to Christ, but because they are no longer using the "tricks of the trade" to attract and even manipulate decisions, their attendance numbers are not nearly as impressive.

Then there's the rural church near a Bible college. They believe that their calling is to take on students as their interim ministers. They give these student ministers love and a place to hone skills and gather experience. Then, rather than holding on to the young minister, they send him off after graduation and take on a new student minister. God is using this congregation, and it's growing the Kingdom—just not in the way we often measure success.

There are house churches and missional congregations who do not emphasize large group gatherings. They are more concerned with their serving and sending capacity than their seating. They may be small in numbers, but they are going, telling, sharing, and showing the world Jesus loves them. They are bearing fruit even though they don't have a building, smoke machines, or moving lights.

We are tempted to forget that God is the one who gives the growth. When we do, we put pressure on ourselves and may feel guilty when things are not going as we had hoped. We reduce success to superficial things like buildings, budgets, and attendance numbers. But often success and Kingdom impact are not measured in such ways. God gives the growth, and our focus should be on seeking Him and faithfully serving His will, leaving the results to Him.

Humans Affect It

With all that being said, it's also important to note that sometimes churches don't have impact because they don't want to. God wants to work through them in a greater way than they are experiencing, but leadership, people, and church culture get in the way. Like Diotrephes in 3 John, they do things to push people away and limit the church's influence (3 John 9-10).

Sometimes it's overt. More often than not it's unintentional. Churches have blind spots and are unknowingly doing things to limit themselves. As G. K. Chesterton once said, "It isn't that they can't see the solution. It's that they can't see the problem."[20] Any seasoned consultant can walk into a church environment and see things from the outside which may be hurting that church. In most cases, it's not obvious to the people involved that they are hurting themselves and hindering their ability to communicate the gospel and impact people.

Every church I've ever talked to has told me that they want to reach more people, but in reality, most aren't willing to do what may be necessary. Some would rather just shift the blame to God by saying that it's not His will. Others would rather blame the church down the street, Hollywood, or the fact that young people today aren't as committed as they used to be. These people do ministry with blinders on, unable to discern their own culpability.

The story in Acts 6 points out that as the leaders sought the Lord and made a practical and spiritual decision to make the church healthier, the congregation saw greater impact. You will never convince me that God would have blessed them in such a measure if the apostles had buried their heads in the sand and neglected the problem, allowing division and discrimination to flourish in Jerusalem, or if they had taken on the extra responsibility themselves, neglecting the elements of ministry that only they could do.

Yes, God is the one who makes the church grow. And not every church is
called to be large or increasing in size. Yet far too often, poor leadership,
apathetic church members, denial, and an unspoken desire for a holy huddle
are what hinder the church's ability to reach more people for Christ.

Being part of an impacting church is an exciting and rewarding adventure.
But make no mistake about it… it comes at a cost. Significant challenges will
pop up and must be addressed, and being unaware of this feeds an idealism
that actually sets the local church up for even greater problems. Growth is
messy and risky. It changes everything, and it requires both divine and human
partnership. When a congregation understands this and embraces it, they
nurture an environment that is conducive for lasting growth and sustainable
impact.

Chapter 8

APPROPRIATE CHANGE

"In the medical world, a clinical definition of death is a body that does not change. Change is life. Stagnation is death. If you don't change, you die. It's that simple. It's that scary." - Len Sweet

The original building at Richwoods Christian Church was about 11,000 square feet with a unique layout. One of the main hallways, which also served as the entry point for the sanctuary, had a little wall that jutted out about three feet, resulting in a fairly useless cubby space. Originally, there was a small table there, and on the wall was a stenciled grapevine with the words "He is the vine and we are the branches." On those vines were Polaroid pictures of all the church members.

As the church grew, it was evident that we had moved beyond the vine and branches, both aesthetically and practically. There were more people joining than we had vine space for. More importantly, though, that area was where we had the entrance to the sanctuary and the check-in for the kids' ministry. It became a real bottleneck.

We decided to knock out the three-foot wall in order to open up hallway space and paint over the vine and branches. This didn't appear to be a major decision. But on the day the wall was being knocked down, I saw one of our founding members standing and watching the work. I strolled down the hallway toward her and noticed that tears were streaming down her face.

I asked, "Jan, are you okay?" She responded by nodding her head and then gently saying, "It's just hard."

This lady was supportive of the direction our church was going and the changes we were making. Yet that cubby space represented memories and history. Changing it brought sadness. What some saw as cheesy, stenciled artwork on the wall had a greater symbolic meaning to her as a founding member. All we were doing was removing a three-foot section of wall, but for this lovely lady, it was still emotional and challenging.

Any church that has a vision for reaching people must understand some things are going to change. Even for supportive people, this can be difficult. And for those who are not on board, it is even more challenging. Therefore, it becomes incumbent for a healthy church to establish a theology of change—a biblical standard for how to approach transitions to help them discern which changes are appropriate and which ones aren't.

Without a biblical philosophy of change, issues are often addressed on a purely emotional level, or people intellectually debate them out of false assumptions and bad theology. Then these discussions usually deteriorate into an unspiritual battle that hurts people, divides the congregation, and hinders their redemptive potential. Here are five principles that represent mindsets associated with a healthy theology of change.

Define Who God Is and How He Interacts

One of the great truths of Scripture is that God is immutable. He does not change (Malachi 3:6; James 1:17; Hebrews 13:8). His very nature, along with His Word, His love, and His promises do not morph, evolve, or fail. The Lord is constant, dependable, and stable. Therefore we can trust Him. He is our rock and fortress.

Yet this great truth leads some to a false conclusion that God is therefore "anti-change." If the Lord doesn't change, then why should we? This becomes a convenient excuse for people to become set in their ways and resistant to anything new or different from what they already feel comfortable with. But as we look into Scripture, we find that God is actually pro-change.

God Changes His Interactions

On several occasions, the Lord made known what He was intending to do, only to modify His plans due to the intercession of people. When Abraham and Moses called out to God, we are told the Lord "relented." He softened His stance and did not execute the judgment He had planned. The prophet Hosea records the Lord saying, *"How can I give you up, Ephraim? How can I hand you over, Israel? My heart is changed within me; all my compassion is aroused. I will not carry out my fierce anger"* (11:8-9).

God Calls People to Change Their Plans

Over and over, we find God calling people out of their comfort zones and into something they did not want to do. Oftentimes people questioned and pushed back on God because they did not want to make the change He was asking them to make. Whether it was Moses being called to Egypt, Gideon to lead an army, or Jeremiah to become a prophet, they were being asked to do something other than what they had planned to do with their lives.

God Allows People to Drive Change

God doesn't always initiate change. Sometimes He allows people to do something for Him and in His name. Basically, God gives them the freedom, and often His blessing, to make something happen. Nehemiah desired to return home and rebuild the walls of Jerusalem. David desired to build a temple. In each case they were taking initiative to do something for the Lord. God didn't specifically call them or directly tell them they had to do it, but He allowed them to act on what they had in their hearts. For Nehemiah, that meant actually doing the project. For David, the Lord did not allow him to build the temple, but He permitted David to plan and prepare for Solomon to do so. In each case God blessed and gave favor, even though He did not directly initiate the projects.

God Endorses the New and Different

Three times in the book of Isaiah alone the Lord speaks of doing "new things" (Isaiah 43:18-19). In the New Testament we read about a new law, new birth, new heaven, new earth, new life, new teaching, new creation, new command, new self, new Jerusalem, new name, new covenant, new regulations, new order, and a new way. The second to the last chapter in the Bible states that Jesus is "making all things new" (Revelation 21:5). To think that God lives in the past and is most concerned with keeping things as they are is almost laughable.

God Expects Us to Change

The Lord has an overarching desire to see us grow and mature, becoming increasingly more like Jesus. The Bible uses words like repent, convert, turn, renew, revive, restore, and transform to describe how He calls both the lost and the saved to adjust their lives. God loves us right where we are, but He doesn't want us to stay there. He is constantly calling us to grow, change, and mature.

Yes, God is immutable. Yet over and over again the Bible shows us God is still very much pro-change. We have to help the church understand the difference between God's nature and His involvement with people. Without understanding the difference, we can falsely believe that we should dig in our heels on issues that God may be trying to address.

Taste and Truth

Wheaties cereal was introduced in 1924. About ten years later, the company began to develop one of the most successful marketing campaigns ever by placing athletes on the cover of their cereal boxes. Even today, Wheaties uses this same strategy to effectively market their product. It's important to note that the recipe for Wheaties is the same today as it was when it was introduced. But the faces on the box are different: Lou Gehrig, Bruce Jenner, Mary Lou Retton, and Michael Jordan are no longer used to sell the cereal. The cover is always changing, even though the content isn't.

This same principle carries over to the church. The box is much like the forms or methods of how we communicate the gospel. They are always in flux and vary among cultures and generations. The truth of the gospel is the content—it should remain fixed. There is a difference between methodology and theology. Between traditions and truth. Yet I am still amazed at how easy it is for us to confuse the two.

A healthy theology of change makes a clear distinction between methods (which are always changing) and the message (which shouldn't change). It defines and illustrates for the congregation what things are matters of liberty and what things are not.

For example, I can preach a sermon wearing a variety of outfits. I can preach wearing a suit and tie. I can preach in a robe. I can preach in khakis or in dress jeans. I can preach in shorts and a tie-dyed shirt. Does one outfit make me more spiritual than another? Does the exact same sermon become more or less true based upon the outfit I wear? The content of my sermon is a matter of truth; what kind of clothes I wear when I preach is a matter of taste. When I preach in my grandparents' Lutheran church, a robe is appropriate. If I'm preaching at an ocean front church in Hawaii, a tie-dyed shirt may be in order. The context is different, and, therefore, my attire may change in order to better relate to my audience. But the message is still the same.

One generation argues over whether it's appropriate to have electricity and plumbing in the church building. The next generation debates whether it's appropriate to have projectors and screens. The next questions whether it's even necessary to have a building at all. Methodology, forms, and style vary from culture to culture and from generation to generation. Matters of truth should remain constant.

Go all the way back to Jesus, and you'll find that part of the reason the Pharisees missed Christ is because He would not follow all of their man-made traditions. The Pharisees had blurred the line between tradition and truth to the point that they failed to see Jesus. If we don't define the difference between issues of taste and truth, we are in danger of limiting our ability to effectively communicate the gospel to an ever-changing, ever-evolving world.

Relevance

In my first church, we had a lady named Fran who was reading through a bunch of old documents from our congregation. She came across the minutes from a congregational meeting in the 1920s that detailed a growing divide among the church members. The "young families" wanted to start using the organ in the actual worship service, but the "older members" were opposed. It was decided that they would allow the organ to be used during the Sunday school hour, but not during church services.

Seventy years later, we were only using the organ in worship, except on occasions when we didn't have anyone to play it. When a couple of young families and I suggested that we incorporate the piano and guitar into the worship service, some of the "older members" were opposed to it. Not all, but some. The instruments had changed. The generation was different. The hesitancy to adapt was the same.

Times change, as do preferences and styles. Being relevant is simply taking the message of the gospel and communicating it in a way that is applicable to that generation or society. Most missionaries get this. They realize that if they are going to a foreign country to serve God and they want to be effective, they need to learn the language and customs of the people. If I'm in Peru but don't speak Spanish or have a translator, I'm probably not going to be very successful, no matter how well-intentioned my motives are.

Society is changing at a rapid rate. Many leaders in local churches are two or three generations removed from today's young adults and are hesitant to adjust their methods or give a voice to that generation. Len Sweet, who graduated from seminary in 1969, said, "I was trained to do ministry in a world that no longer exists." If we fail to acknowledge this, we are tempted to hold to things that once worked but no longer connect with young adults.

This is being lived out in a huge shift between the Baby Boomers and the generations behind them. In the 1980s and '90s, one of the values emphasized in leadership and church growth literature was the importance of being "excellent." Boomers valued this and even demanded it. Many had been raised in churches where things were thrown together and shoddy, yet in all other areas of their lives, they were experiencing a level of quality that they had never seen in the church.

Many churches made the shift and began to raise their level of excellence, and it worked in attracting Boomers. But today is a new day. Teenagers and young adults now value authenticity over excellence. As a matter of fact, if things are too polished, this generation often interprets that as being manipulative and fake. What once was helping make the gospel more relevant to one generation has become a barrier in connecting with the next.

In the Old Testament, we read about a group of people who understood the importance of relevance—*"the men of Issachar understood the times and knew what Israel should do"* (1 Chronicles 12:32). Being relevant means that we grasp the age in which we live, and rather than holding on to the past, we evaluate the present culture in light of our calling and contextualize the gospel to more effectively reach the lost.

This is a continual process. Society is always in motion—now more than ever.

Name Your Islands

The premise of Alvin Toffler's 1970 book *Future Shock* was that society was about to see an enormous amount of rapid change on multiple fronts. In this book Toffler coined the term "information overload" because he felt people were going to be overwhelmed with the rate and amount of change they would face. As a result, people would feel disconnected and sense that nothing is permanent anymore.

Toffler's prediction was spot on. Yet he didn't just present the problem; he also advocated some solutions to help people navigate this transition. One solution he called for was providing people with "stability zones." Stability zones are things that help people relax, enabling them to feel safe and secure even though things around them are in flux. These stability zones can be people, ideas, objects, or places.

Part of the problem churches face is that many people are freaked out and emotionally unsettled by the speed and onslaught of an ever-changing world. Without even realizing it, they want to be able to walk into a church and find a stability zone. A place that doesn't change. An environment that is consistent and reliable… because little else in their world appears to be.

Several years ago, a colleague in ministry told me about a board member of his church who also happened to be an executive of a Fortune 500 company. The board member was a forward thinker at his job and often expressed frustration over the slowness in which his company moved. Yet almost every time the church board would talk about changing things in the congregation, this same man would become negative and resistant. One day the pastor confronted the situation. The executive acknowledged the inconsistency between how he approached his job and how he approached his role as a board member in the church. He said, "I deal with change all the time on my job. I just don't have the energy to deal with it at the church."

In order to help people who are overwhelmed and to prevent them from hurting the church's potential, we must proactively try to define our "stability zones." We must determine what things besides the gospel message will *not* change. These things can be doctrinal beliefs, behaviors, or values. There is no right or wrong list. The main thing is that something is defined.

For us at Richwoods, this includes our essential doctrinal positions and some practical aspects of ministry, such as the practice of believer baptism. We also serve communion every week in our corporate worship services. These beliefs and practices are part of our history, and they serve as islands that people can drift to in the midst of rocky seas. If a person doesn't agree with our essential doctrinal statement or doesn't like the fact that we serve communion weekly, there are hundreds of other churches in our area for them to attend. But these are convictions that we have, and they are islands of stability. They give our core members something to hang on to even though many other elements of our church are in transition. This gives the leadership an enormous amount of freedom to know that outside of those islands, we have great latitude to tweak, change, and adjust what we do and how we are doing it.

A Shot in the Dark

Sometimes you have to be willing to try something without the guarantee of success. Church consultant Sam Chand says that a healthy organization almost always develops a "culture of experimentation," a willingness to try new things with the understanding that they might not work out.[21]

Churches with a healthy theology of change almost always embrace a mindset that is comfortable with some measure of mistakes and failure. They take strategic risks. They try new things. And if those new things don't work out, they debrief, learn, sometimes laugh, and move forward. They're not trying to make mistakes, but they don't snap or overreact if an idea fails.

Peter was the only apostle to step out of the boat. He took his eyes off Jesus and started to sink. Yet we hail Peter for his faith and his willingness to take a risk and move toward Jesus when everyone else was too scared. We also know that the apostle Paul was a man of great faith, but he didn't succeed every time he walked into a community and preached the gospel. Furthermore, on two occasions he tried to take the gospel north and east only to have the door close and God redirect him to Macedonia (Acts 16:6-9). His heart was in the right place, and he was trying to advance the gospel to reach lost people in Asia, but ultimately, it wasn't God's plan. He kept trying, but God said, "No."

An old adage says, "It's always easier to steer a car when it's moving." Sometimes when we wonder if something will work, we just need to try it and see. And then we need to be okay if it doesn't. If failure is not an option, then neither is success.

I'm not advocating recklessness or immature optimism. Nor am I suggesting that we shouldn't be willing to wait on the Lord. We need to be prayerful. Strategic. Realistic. We must count the cost. Yet we also need to break out of the mold, follow our hearts, take a risk, and do something to try to further the gospel. As Rick Warren says, "You cannot succeed in ministry by avoiding failure. You must obediently take risks in faith."[22]

If a congregation wants to reach an ever-changing world, they must contextualize the gospel and be flexible in their methodology and presentation.

They must be willing to move beyond threadbare programming or the status quo.

When leaders take the time to establish and teach a theology of change, they lay a foundation on which more acceptance, openness, and support for the new can be built. This frees the church to adjust traditions, initiatives, and programs without compromising truth. It serves to loosen the soil and create fertile bedding that promotes healthy growth.

Chapter 9

PERPETUAL FORMATION

"The revolution of Jesus is in the first place and continuously a revolution of the human heart and spirit." – Dallas Willard

Shortly after getting my first smart phone, I came across a new and addicting game. It was challenging and multi-layered, with various levels and achievements. It took me several months of intense practice, but eventually I was able to beat it. I finished the adventure and unlocked and completed all the special achievements, as well as the secondary games associated with it. While friends were still struggling to beat the game, I was able to gloat with a subtle sense of pride that I had conquered it.

Several months later, I noticed one of my children playing the same game. He was doing something I had never seen before, so I asked him what was going on. He explained that he had downloaded some recent upgrades and that the game now included new levels and achievements. I immediately thought, *Oh man, I thought I had that game beaten, but it looks like I've now got more work to do.*

I downloaded the upgrade and for several weeks intensely pursued my new goal of beating the new levels so that I could once again experience the satisfaction of achievement. Several months later, a new upgrade came out, and the process started all over again.

Then one day a thought occurred to me. The way that I approached this game is the way I am tempted to approach spiritual maturity. I am often hyper-focused on selected areas of my life. I work hard to conquer and fix things that are broken, and if I'm fortunate enough to notice progress, I am tempted to stand back with a subtle pride—feeling as if I have arrived.

This tendency was revealed when I visited a friend who happens to be a professional counselor. During our conversation, he asked me what I did with my anger. I explained to him that I didn't have a problem with anger anymore. When I was younger, I had a bad temper, but I memorized verses, prayed diligently, and worked hard to exercise self-control. I shared a couple of stories to illustrate how I responded in a good way in situations where previously I might have blown up. My friend then raised his eyebrows and rather sarcastically said, "So you're telling me you don't have any more anger in your life?"

The next several minutes were embarrassing as my friend exposed the blindness and denial that were present inside my heart.

I'm still prone to see spiritual maturity as a series of accomplishments and to believe I'm farther along than I really am. I am also tempted to prop myself up by comparing my life with others' lives. Yet in spite of this, God is transforming my understanding of spiritual formation—not only in my own life, but also in the life of the church body. Discipleship and spiritual growth are at the heart of God's will for the body of Christ, and if we are not emphasizing this in a healthy way, we are failing to nurture a good culture and thereby limiting God.

Tie Everything to Spiritual Growth

One of the ways we limit God's ability to bless the church is when we do things unintentionally that disassociate individual growth from the overall mission and activities of the congregation. When people come, we ask them to serve in a ministry, and we talk about programs, activities, worship services, and events. Then, when we talk about spiritual formation, we generally change the conversation to sermons, classes, books, and group life. When we do this, we send a poor message that can stunt people's growth and hurt the overall redemptive mission of the church. In reality, we should be attempting to tie everything that occurs in and through the church to personal growth.

The writer of Hebrews understood this and emphasized the marriage of service and spiritual formation in his closing prayer:

> *"Now may the God of peace who brought again from the dead our Lord Jesus, the great shepherd of the sheep, by the blood of the eternal covenant, equip you with everything good that you may do his will, working in us that which is pleasing in his sight, through Jesus Christ, to whom be glory forever and ever. Amen."* Hebrews 13:20-21

This verse is a call to action and mission—the things we need to do in order to live our faith and complete the calling God has given us. Faith—true faith—is accompanied by action. Therefore, the writer of Hebrews prays that God will "equip you with everything good for doing His will." The word translated "equip" is *kataritzo*, and it speaks about making something complete, perfect, or fully adequate. It was used in Greek literature to describe the setting of a broken bone, the mending of fishing nets, and the outfitting of a ship for a voyage.

So, the author is praying that God will give you everything you need to complete and fulfill His will for your life. He will give you the strength, the desire, the opportunity, the ability, the power, the fortitude, the wisdom, and the resources that you need, so you can perform and carry out whatever it is that He wants you to do. But the writer doesn't stop there. He adds something to his prayer that I fear is not emphasized enough in modern day Christianity: "work in us what is pleasing to Him."

There are a couple of things worth noting here. First of all, "work" is a present tense verb, which means that it's an action in process with no real completion. In other words, the author is asking God to work in us and to continue working in us because God's internal work will never be completed until we reach heaven.

Secondly, there is a significant change in pronoun. Earlier the author says, "equip *you*," but here he says "work in *us*." Some translations use the pronoun "you" in both halves of the verse for continuity, but in the Greek the latter pronoun is first person plural, whereas the former is second person singular. The reason for this is that we all need God to equip us in unique ways because He leads and calls us to do different things. But when it comes to God working in us, the intended purpose is universal.

And what is the purpose of God working in us? To do "what is pleasing to Him." And what is pleasing to Him is our internal transformation whereby God aligns, not only our actions, but also our thoughts, motives, ambitions, values, and beliefs to be like those of Jesus. God wants to conform our entire being into the image of His Son—renovating our hearts, renewing our minds, and making us more like Christ.

At the baptism of Jesus, the Father spoke from heaven that He was "well pleased" with the Son (Matthew 3:17). The Father's pleasure was rooted in the character of Jesus, not just what He was doing. Jesus had not yet preached to the lost, healed the sick, confronted the Pharisees, or gone to the cross. Yet the Father delighted in Jesus because of *who* Jesus was. And the Father wants to work *in us* in order to make us more holy, righteous, and Christlike so that He can take delight in *who* we are as well. Obviously, we are already cleansed through Jesus' blood, but the Lord wants to make our position in Christ a real-time reality by making us more like Jesus in this lifetime. This is ultimately what is most pleasing to God—our sanctification.

Therefore, it's essential for leaders to give the church body a vision of God continually working in us, even as He works through us. This means that everything we do inside and outside the church is tied to God moving us toward spiritual maturity. Thus our fatigue, relational conflict, criticism, disappointment, and anything else that occurs are all connected to something deeper and richer—our spiritual formation.

Keep It Clear

In the midst of all the activities in the church, God is continually working to make us increasingly more like Jesus. As Bonhoeffer said, "God became like man, that man may become like God." This is not just a positional statement referring to our relationship with God through Christ; it's also a practical statement that speaks to the end goal for all Christians.

The Scriptures use a variety of words and phrases to emphasize this: be conformed to the image of Christ (Romans 8:29); grow up into Him (Ephesians 4:15); allow Christ to be formed in you (Galatians 4:19); be fully mature in Him (Colossians 1:28); be imitators of God (Ephesians 5:1); be perfect (Matthew 5:48); be holy (1 Peter 1:15); be blameless (Philippians 2:15); be godly (1 Timothy 4:7); be righteous (James 2:24), and live as Jesus lived (1 John 2:6). Jesus did not command us to follow a code of behavior, and He didn't give us a simple and trite definition of spiritual maturity. Rather, He said, "follow me" (Luke 14:27); walk in my steps; do as I do; think like I think; value what I value.

The goal of all these commands is to help people see the importance of becoming Christlike. This is God's overarching purpose for every Christian, and it should be the intended goal of discipleship.

As Jesus stated in the Sermon on the Mount and in His exhortation to the Pharisees (Matthew 23), God wants to do more than just forge behavior, beliefs, and religious activity, no matter how well-intentioned. He wants to transform our hearts, molding all aspects of our lives to be like Him. And what was Jesus like?

> Jesus didn't just live a holy life—he *was* holy.
> Jesus didn't just do righteous actions—he *was* righteous.

When we lay this vision in front of people, it reminds them that everything that happens in and through their lives, as well as in and through the church, is part of God working to make us more like Jesus. Without this emphasis, we tend to compartmentalize the work of the church, doing things *for* God apart from God working in us. We can get caught up doing ministry and works of service to the point that we forget God's greatest and most desired work is to make us more like Christ.

We separate being from doing.

As a result, we can justify attitudes, minimize relational sin, and go off on tangents while doing the work of ministry. We can hold on to pride. We can be defensive and argumentative. We can enable our control issues or yield to our fears and play it safe. Without maintaining a focus on perpetual spiritual formation, our flesh runs wild, and we never confront it. Never repent. Never hold ourselves or others accountable. All the while, we are meeting, singing, praying, preaching, and trying to do the work of the church, never addressing the deeper issues that prevent us from maturing in Christ.

Therefore, we must remind people that in the midst of all the exhortations in Scripture and all the good works we are doing, the primary thing God wants to do in us is to make us more like His Son. We must keep this truth simple and remind the congregation to stay focused on that goal in the midst of all the noise that life and ministry present.

Make It Overwhelming

Once we make the end goal of Christlikeness clear, we then must work to make it overwhelming. We all need a vision of Christlikeness that is so large we realize we will never fully be like Jesus in this lifetime. We need to be reminded that we still need Jesus as much today as we did when we first came to faith in God. Too often, over time and with age, we can subtly begin to feel God has cleaned us up enough that we're doing okay. After all, we're not doing all the foolish stuff we did several years ago, and we've obviously matured as a people, so we're actually doing well.

But is this really the case? When we understand that God's redemptive work includes not only our doctrinal beliefs and moral actions, but also our inner worlds, then we see that we are still broken, sinful, and desperately need God! This keeps us humble. And God blesses humility.

But we avoid brokenness. We associate it with bad circumstances. Even though Martin Luther addressed the subject of having a continually contrite and repentant attitude in the first of his ninety-five theses, many church leaders feel no need to talk about it. We would rather reduce the Kingdom to doctrinal truth, missional actions, or external morality and the like. When we do talk about repentance, we generally do so in the context of salvation rather than sanctification.

We can also be too focused on showing people biblical principles in order to help them fix their lives. As a result, we can lead them to self-sufficiency, teaching them in the process that if they can just balance their checkbooks, get their bodies in shape, worship more consistently, pray daily, etc., they'll be happier and will fulfill God's intention for their lives. I'm not opposed to helping people better manage their lives. I actually want that to occur. But simply carving out a good life on earth is not the end goal. And in some cases, it can actually distract us from the bigger vision of being transformed into Christlikeness.

Jesus did not give us a precise definition of spiritual maturity for a reason. He knew a clear definition would lead to an Old Testament works mentality and would move us away from relationship. Additionally, it would lead to more striving and self-justification, not to mention pride, and it would feed our need to maintain control rather than trust. So, Jesus did not give us an exact definition. What He did do was model and teach a broad and holistic picture of what it looks like to be godly.

In my opinion, our spiritual lives tend to fall into seven dimensions. Each of these categories is biblical in nature and carries extreme value. They are *all* important. They are indicators, but they do not stand alone. Nor do they represent a comprehensive definition of Christlikeness. When taken as a whole, these seven categories give us some insight into what it means to live like and to be like Jesus.

The Devotional. One aspect of Christlikeness is reflected in habits and acts of piety that point to our devotion and are meant to bring us into a closer relationship with the Lord. These include, but are not limited to, prayer, Scripture reading, corporate worship, fasting, giving, and serving. These are not ends in and of themselves, but they are practices that are meant to be a means by which we can honor and know God.

The Intellectual. Another aspect is the intellectual, stretching our minds to increase our understanding of theology, Scripture, and the nature of God. It also includes the knowledge of how to apply what we are learning to our everyday lives and our interactions with others. The bottom line is that we are engaging our minds and allowing our beliefs and thoughts to be shaped and modeled to reflect God's Word and will.

The Behavioral. Actions matter, and we are called to live in obedience to God's commands, leadings, moral precepts, and will. Some behaviors are sinful and need to be avoided; others are righteous and need to be practiced. Jesus said that if we love Him, we will obey Him, and so our actions reflect our hearts and our faith (John 14:15).

The Missional. Jesus came to proclaim the good news, and He calls us to do the same (Matthew 28:19-20). This is engaging in issues of justice, serving the poor, and sharing our faith. It is joining God in His redemptive work to model and proclaim the eternal gospel message to a lost, dying, and hurting world.

The Experiential. The Lord came and displayed His message, not only in words, but also in supernatural displays of His power and by means of a personal relationship with the Father. He told us we would also see signs of His presence and activity in our time (John 14:12). When we walk in a relationship with God, there should be subjective, and even mystical, aspects of our faith that are seen, experienced, and lived through the Holy Spirit. This can be described as experiencing God's presence, hearing His voice, or sensing His leading.

The Relational. The most often overlooked and neglected indicator of spiritual maturity is manifested in our relationships. Relational interactions are perhaps the most emphasized by Jesus and the New Testament (John 13:34-35). This is living out the richness of what God is doing in our lives, based on how we love, forgive, and relate to other people. It is the most ignored and undervalued because it is the hardest to measure; it's impossible to master, and it's frustrating because we can't control other people. Trying to love like Jesus makes us vulnerable, exposes our insecurities, reveals our self-obsession, and still may result in nails and a cross.

The Internal. God is just as concerned with our hearts as He is with our deeds, doctrine, and actions. The internal aspect of our faith speaks to our inner world—where God is attempting to mold our thoughts, attitudes, values, will, and emotions to reflect Christ. The Lord wants to make our private world—the unspoken recesses of our lives—just as Christlike as He wants our external actions to be.

All seven of these dimensions are taught in Scripture and were modeled by Jesus. Each is a challenge. Combined, they seem over the top.

One time when I was preaching on these seven dimensions, a guy in my church approached me and said, "Jim, this is overwhelming. There is no way I can do all of that. I think I'm failing in each of those seven areas, and the thought of trying to live out all of them is just too much for me." I told him, "That's the point. Being like Jesus is overwhelming, and we will never fully achieve perfection in this lifetime. But in our failures we come to see the richness of God's grace, forgiveness, and love."

Having a wide, deep, and complex vision for Christlikeness keeps us humble and reminds us we need God desperately. Instead of causing pressure and bondage, a pursuit of Christlikeness leads to freedom. Because when we run to Jesus, acknowledging how much we fall short, we find once again that by His grace, He loves us, forgives us, and accepts us. This cycle of repentance and grace moves us to know Him, love Him, and serve Him more humbly.

But too often we are scared to come to grips with how ungodly we really are. We don't want to acknowledge our brokenness and would rather focus on the good actions and orthodox beliefs that make us feel worthy. Therefore, we construct ways to make us feel better about our spirituality.

How We Mess It Up

There are several ways we subtly mess up our view of discipleship. As a result, those blind spots hinder our testimony and leave us with a vision for Christlikeness that is short of what God intended. They not only cheat God, but they rob us as well.

Complacency

One of the most prevalent issues is a lack of desire and motivation. Far too often we are content in believing we are going to heaven and are only concerned with living at ease in Zion. When this happens, we can settle for a performance-based spirituality that is satisfied with a saving faith and a manageable life. We are content with "good enough" Christianity and with what Dallas Willard calls "sin management."

At other times, rather than embracing our brokenness and moving towards God, we run like Adam and Eve. We hide from God, believing change is not possible, and we allow shame and guilt to justify the distance. Regardless of what drives it, lethargy, blindness, or fear can keep us from moving toward growth.

Narrowing the Definition

Another way we water down Christlikeness is when we attempt to define spiritual maturity in terms that are manageable and safe. Often it results in a definition that plays to our strengths and passions. It is based on some biblical truth but is not comprehensive enough. Usually, we gravitate toward one or two of the categories I listed above and compartmentalize them by focusing on those areas while underemphasizing or ignoring the others. Let me share some examples of this behavior.

The thinker defines growth in terms of intellectual knowledge but downplays the relational aspects of our faith as being unnecessary or "touchy-feely." So, while she pours herself into books and Bible studies, her marriage crumbles, and her kids walk away. But as long as she is learning Greek words or other tidbits of information about the Bible, she is confident that she's a mature believer and the relational turmoil in her life has nothing to do with her faith.

An experiential person regularly talks about how God is speaking to his heart and how the Lord is directing and guiding him. Yet a lack of discipline or blatant moral sin can be rationalized by saying, "The Lord told me it was okay for me." If there are feelings and experiences linked to God, then that becomes a sign of the Lord's favor, and sin can be justified.

Another person prioritizes the importance of duty and acts of devotion. This person attends church every Sunday, tithes on the gross of her salary, volunteers as a greeter, and reads the Bible every day of the year. These ritualistic observances allow her to compartmentalize her faith into nothing more than duties and checked boxes. Consequently, she can avoid other aspects of her life, such as the misuse of prescription drugs, her short temper, or her regular use of expletives around the house.

The activist focuses on morality and causes. He abhors drunkenness, prostitution, homosexuality, and abortion. He is angered and appalled by hypocrisy. He blogs, pickets, and puts bumper stickers on his car. He is quick to tell the world how sinful these actions are. Yet in his zeal for truth, he turns people away from Jesus because of his pride, judgmental attitude, and inability to speak in love.

Once we define spiritual maturity in terms that we are comfortable with, either formally or informally, we can control it and, in some cases, perfect it. As a result, we look at ourselves in the mirror, pat ourselves on the back, and celebrate how mature and godly we are. We then avoid, rationalize, and continue to be in denial about the other issues in our lives that are broken and out of order.

Lack of Awareness

Another area we struggle in is the ability or desire to honestly examine our lives. We are aware of our obvious problems, such as peeking at pornography, drinking too much at the Christmas party, or refusing to forgive our abusers. But we avoid self-reflection when it comes to the daily battles with our flesh that occur moment by moment, day after day.

This is marked by the lack of confession in many of our prayer times, and when we do confess things, we bring up the same things again and again, often addressing them in generalities: "Lord, forgive me for my pride and my greed." This is a good start, but still shallow. When walking in a conscious awareness of our depravity, we ought to be more aware of the real-time sin we face—not just our external actions, but also the deeper issues of our hearts. This means not just confessing our general struggle with lust, but rather, acknowledging specifics—the fantasy we entertained while driving the car, the magazine photo that we dwelt on, or the waitress we were "checking out" at the restaurant.

Linear Growth

A final way to mess up our vision of growth involves how we view the process. We all understand that the shortest distance between two points is a straight line. But if you've ever hiked in the Rocky Mountains, you know that a straight line isn't always possible, nor is it always best. Unfortunately, we've been conditioned to think that a straight line is the best way to achieve spiritual growth. We are here. We want to go there. So, let's develop a formula, program, or some incremental steps in order to help us reach our destination. Sometimes this does, in fact, help. The problem with this is that true learning usually occurs in waves and in more of a circular fashion than a linear one. We learn something, forget about it, struggle with it, and then it cycles back around. We then hopefully re-learn it or apply it in a deeper manner. Attempting linear growth leads us toward a formulaic, industrialized spirituality that is trite and shallow.

Connecting It to the Congregation

Each of these patterns limits our ability to grow to our full potential in Christ. They are often born out of a desire to control our spirituality, to justify ourselves, and to be able to positively compare ourselves to those around us. When limiting mindsets are systematically held to by a congregation, whether intentionally or not, they hinder individual growth, and they stunt the maturation of the entire congregation.

When this occurs, as individuals and as a congregation, we are not developing as God intends. We lack the maturity to take the church where it needs to go. We are incapable of making the necessary sacrifices—dying to self, losing our lives, and loving the lost. Passive-aggressive behavior, scorekeeping, and other petty attitudes become the norm for relational interaction and result in disunity and bickering.

On the other hand, when we have a clear, overwhelming vision for Christlikeness that ties everything to spiritual formation, we are laying the foundation for God to mature us as individuals and as a community. We'll come to see we are just as broken and in need of God's grace today as we've ever been. When this happens, humility is prevalent; spiritual growth is occurring, and God is pleased. And when God is pleased, God blesses. He will bless the work of our hands, and He will make us more like Himself in the process. This is a win-win.

Section 3
THE APPLICATION

Chapter 10

ENVISIONING YOUR HARVEST

*"To the person who does not know where he wants to
go there is no favorable wind."* - Seneca

Before I took over as the minister at Richwoods, I began to receive their monthly newsletter in the mail. If you've ever been part of a small church, you understand about the newsletter. It has several pages of personal information about members, serving schedules, announcements, and a short article. But there was something about this newsletter that got my attention. At the top, centered and highlighted, was this verse:

> *"The Lord's hand was with them, and a great number of people
> believed and turned to the Lord."* Acts 11:21

The next month I got another newsletter, and the same verse was present. And then the next month, and the next, and the next...

I thought to myself, *How cool is this?* I was impressed that a struggling church facing serious questions about whether they would have to close their doors was still holding to a belief that God's hand was upon them and that He was going to do great things through them.

The church had a dream. It just hadn't discovered its calling.

A Calling

A calling is an invitation from God. It is more than a program, a person, a building, or isolated actions. It is a summons to a way of life.

It's not confined to beliefs or methodology, and it's certainly not the same thing as a leading. We often confuse leadings with a calling. But a calling is larger and all encompassing, whereas a leading is specific and contained within the larger plan.

The Lord led the Israelites out of Egypt and called them to be a holy and distinct people. He wanted them to trust Him and to establish themselves in the Holy Land He had promised. He sent a person named Moses and used a cloud by day and a pillar of fire by night to guide them. God was clearly at work in their midst, and He was obviously leading them. However, He led them in circles. Around and around the desert they went because of their refusal to trust, to believe, and to embrace God's bigger vision. So, an entire generation of Israelites never got where God wanted them to go. They were living in the moment, and God was leading them. Yet they never understood that God's calling was much larger than what they could see from day to day.

Churches still do the same thing today. Often they come across a new idea and say, "God is calling us to do this." In reality, the Lord may in fact be opening a door or leading them in a new direction, but if they don't understand this leading within the framework of a larger calling, they will likely not bear as much fruit as God intends. As a result, they are often found searching the horizon, looking for the next thing they are supposed to do, only to see limited results before trying something else.

Without a calling, a church looks like …

An octopus on rollerblades

A ship without a rudder

A kite without a string

They have lots of movement and all kinds of activity. But, ultimately, they are flailing with little or no forward progress.

Conversely, when churches are able to discern what God is "calling" them to do and be, everything changes. They have more unity, greater focus, and a broader sense of purpose. They are more discerning regarding what to engage in and what to refuse. And when they live within their calling, they experience the freedom to resist the pull of the latest fad or to replicate what the growing church down the street is doing. In addition, they usually see more long-term fruit and are honoring God's specific purpose for their body.

Rather than turning inward and succumbing to spiritual entropy, a church with a calling is continually pushing the people's attention upward, outward, and forward. As it pertains to the subject of this book, once you know what your church's calling is, you have the foundation to better discern what values need to be cultivated into the life of the congregation in order to facilitate an environment where you can live out that calling.

On the Front End

When you think about farmers planting a crop, it is essential to understand that different seeds thrive in different environments. After all, you don't see many cornfields in Arizona, and you don't see coconut trees in Minnesota. What is able to grow and flourish in one environment may not be successful in another.

Obviously, when we think about the parable of the sower, there is only one seed—the gospel of Jesus. But remember the seed's success is contingent upon the soil, or environment in which it's planted. The premise stated in Chapter 1 was that a church with a calling could see greater potential for Kingdom impact if the right values are injected into its congregational culture. But if you don't have a vision for what God is calling your church to be and do, it's hard to know what kind of values need to be emphasized.

For example, if your church is located in a liberal university town, you will likely have a slightly different set of values than a rural church located in a conservative part of the country. Both churches need to sow the same seed (the gospel of Jesus), but the mindsets of the people inside and outside those churches are going to be vastly different. By taking this into consideration, churches are able to more appropriately discern what values are essential to developing a culture that will enable the gospel to bear fruit.

So, it becomes imperative to first seek the Lord for a clear sense of calling, a working knowledge of what He is asking your church to do and be.

The Facets

A calling can be simple, or it can be complex. It can be short-term or for a lifetime. It can come in a moment, or it can evolve over time. It can be narrow or broad. But the churches that have the clearest sense of calling and the greatest impact usually have clarity in the following areas:

What They Are Doing

Knowing what you are called to do is often defined within some form of a mission statement. It is always action-oriented, and it pinpoints what the congregation is going to primarily focus on doing. In most cases, it's short, concise, and clear. At Richwoods, our mission statement is "Helping people find and follow Christ," which means working to help people come into a relationship with God (Salvation) and then moving them toward growth and maturity in Christ (Discipleship). There are hundreds of mission statements that are all worded differently. The main thing is that the statement is real, believed, and drives the activity of the church.

Where They Are Going

When a congregation has an idea of where they are headed, it is usually stated within a vision statement. Just as God gave the Israelites vivid images of the Promised Land, a vision statement should paint a picture of a preferable future. If the congregation keeps doing what they are doing, this is where they see God taking them. Many vision statements include measurable or tangible outcomes. Others are more artistic. All should burn an image in the mind and strive to make that image a reality. The bottom line is that a church with a calling has an idea of where they believe God wants them to go and the kind of long-term impact they believe God wants them to have.

Whom They Are Reaching

Knowing the people your church is primarily focused on reaching is most generally referred to as a target audience. A lot of churches I encounter feel uncomfortable talking about this. They feel their job is to reach everyone and they should not limit God by trying to narrow their focus and possibly offend or alienate someone. But this is naïve in a diverse and pluralistic society.

Every church I've ever walked into has a target audience. If you look at the architecture, the way people dress, how they talk, and what kind of music they play, you can quickly get a good idea of the kind of person that church is going to attract.

One time when I spoke of this, a woman who had recently moved to our area told me her story. She said her family had visited over fifteen churches trying to find the right one for her family. She concluded her story by saying, "We got to the point that we could get a feel for a church just by pulling into the parking lot. When we saw lots of Buicks, dresses, and suits, it was an older crowd and more traditional worship. Mini-vans, SUVs, and jeans meant it was more casual and modern. When we saw a disproportionate number of luxury cars, it was an affluent church and generally more aloof."

It's crazy for a church to think they are going to be relevant to all people and reach them equally. That's like saying a satellite company only needs to offer one channel in order to be successful. Society has never been more diverse, and a church with a strong sense of calling knows the types of people they are primarily trying to reach. Then they target their ministry to that group, understanding that they are not going to appeal to everyone. This does not mean that they are exclusive; it just means they are deliberate, wise, and focused.

What Their Niche Is

Shortly after I started at Richwoods, a family that had just moved to town visited the church, and I asked them to lunch. The husband and wife were both Bible college grads who had been in ministry for several years. The husband decided to leave full-time ministry and go back to school. He had just graduated with his doctorate and was now moving to Peoria to become the new marketing professor at Bradley University.

As we sat down to eat, he asked me if we had clarified our mission and vision. Then he asked me this question: "How is Richwoods going to be unique or what are they going to offer that is different from all the other churches in Peoria?" I was speechless. I stumbled and stammered, then finally acknowledged that I had no clue.

He was asking me about a positioning statement, and people in marketing will tell you it may be the single most important piece of information for a successful organization or business. The church isn't a business, I know. But I think there is something to this idea. Just as the individual church is a body and the members have unique gifts, talents, and abilities that they bring to that congregation (Romans 12; 1 Corinthians 12), I believe the larger body of Christ in your community can function the same way. Imagine the Church ("Big C") in your area, and ask yourself, *What is it that makes our church different and unique from the dozens, or perhaps hundreds, of other congregations in our community?* A church with a clear calling knows how to answer that.

What They Believe

Knowing what your core beliefs are is essential for a healthy church. This means having a clear doctrinal statement and, perhaps, even a philosophy of ministry. A doctrinal statement enumerates what your church believes and what members are required to believe. It usually explains essential and nonessential beliefs, lines of tolerance, and membership requirements. Congregations that know what God is calling them to do and be almost always have a clear definition of beliefs and expectations for their church body.

It's More Biblical Than You Might Think

Some might wonder if such a detailed discussion of a calling is necessary or even biblical. Just a casual look at the apostle Paul from the book of Galatians can help answer that question.

Paul opens his epistle in verse one by clarifying his calling: "Paul, an apostle—sent not with human commission nor by human authority, but by Jesus Christ." Later in chapter one and then again in chapter two, Paul reemphasizes that

God has called him to proclaim the gospel based on his position and duty as an apostle (1:15; 2:2). Paul opens every epistle he individually wrote by stating his authority, saying he was "called by God" (Romans 1:1), "commanded" by God (1 Timothy 1:1), or is an apostle in accordance with "the will of God" (Colossians 1:1). The only epistles that Paul doesn't open in such a fashion are coauthored.

Later in Galatians, after sharing his conversion story, Paul expands on his calling:

> *"On the contrary, they recognized that I had been entrusted with the task of preaching the gospel to the uncircumcised, just as Peter had been to the circumcised. For God, who was at work in Peter as an apostle to the circumcised, was also at work in me as an apostle to the Gentiles. James, Cephas and John, those esteemed as pillars, gave me and Barnabas the right hand of fellowship when they recognized the grace given to me. They agreed that we should go to the Gentiles, and they to the circumcised."* Galatians 2:7-9

First notice that Paul has clarity of mission (what he is doing). He was entrusted with the responsibility of preaching the gospel. Next, Paul lists a target audience (whom he is reaching). He is taking the gospel to the Gentiles. This doesn't mean he excluded Jews, but his main attention was given to reaching the Gentiles. Finally, Paul makes it clear that he understands his unique position within the larger body of Christ (what his niche is). Just as God was using Peter and the other "esteemed pillars" to reach the Jews, Paul and Barnabas were being used to reach the Gentiles. There was cooperation and unity, yet there were differences in whom they were targeting and how they were proclaiming the message.

What is not clearly stated in this passage is a vision (where he was going). But a couple of chapters later, Paul gives one of the most powerful and passionate images in all the Epistles. He says, "I am in the pains of childbirth until Christ is formed in you" (4:19). Paul is giving a detailed picture of what he longs to see happen in the Galatian believers—that they would mature, grow, and develop in Christlikeness.

As for the issue of doctrine (what they believe), the overarching theme and perhaps key element to the entire book of Galatians is that the church was being sucked into a false gospel (1:6). Paul was trying to stabilize them, calling them back to the true message of Jesus.

You Can't Make This Up

I believe that every church has a calling, and that calling comes from God.

It is something to be discovered, not something you choose.[23] Paul didn't choose to be an apostle—God chose Him. And the local church cannot dictate their calling and still be in the center of God's will.

Many people are familiar with the verse, "Where there is no vision, the people perish" (Proverb 29:18 [KJV]). The word "vision" is a translation of the Hebrew word *hazon,* but it is not the best translation. A better translation of *hazon* is "revelation"—something that is revealed directly from God. The same word is used to describe the days when the Word of the Lord was rare and there was no revelation coming from heaven (1 Samuel 3:1; Lamentations 2:9). It is also used when the prophets heard directly from the Lord and shared what they received (Isaiah 1:1; Hosea 12:10). When the prophets spoke for themselves and shared words that were not from God, their prophecies were called "false visions" (Jeremiah 14:14). Are you noticing a theme? In almost every occurrence in the Old Testament, the word *hazon* is used with prophetic overtones that revolve around God as the source and the center.

Therefore, it really doesn't matter what other ministries are doing, how cool it sounds, or how excited you are. If you try to generate a calling yourself... you are destined to fail. A true calling is not a wild dream or something you throw together on a whim.

> You must seek it.
>> You must wait for it.
>>> You must discern it.
>>>> You must get it from God.

How Then?

There are people, and even congregations, who receive their calling in a flash. It comes suddenly, clearly, and powerfully. More often than not, though, it becomes crystallized over time.

I had a dramatic conversion experience when I was twenty years old. I felt an immediate sense of calling, but I didn't know if I was going to be an evangelist, a youth pastor, or a missionary. It was only over time and through a process that God's purpose for my life became clear and specific. I find this is more common than Moses' burning bush experience.

Whether it comes quickly or slowly, the one thing that is absolutely true is there is no formula to discern God's calling. It can't be rushed or manipulated. Yet I do think there are some things you can do to put yourself in a position to better discern it.

Ask the Right Questions

In his book *It,* Craig Groeschel suggests churches wrestle with this series of questions in order to determine what God may be calling them to do: Why does your church exist? What can you be the best in the world at? If you could only do one thing, what would it be? If you left tomorrow, what would you hope would continue forever? What breaks your heart and would keep you awake at night?

Let me add a few more of my own: What is God blessing in and through your congregation? What are you doing that is not working or bearing no fruit? Is there anything that almost everyone in your church would say "yes" to? Is there an unmet need or opportunity that no other church appears to be engaging?

Hang Out

Just as Samuel needed Eli to understand what God was saying, sometimes we need to include people from the congregation in the process. It is a mistake for leaders to work in a vacuum as they try to discern a vision for an entire group of people. My suggestion is to bring the people into it.

Early on, when we were seeking God for our calling and when we revisited our calling a few years later, we did several things I think were helpful. We had all our leaders read and discuss a book on the subject.[24] We surveyed the congregation. We brought in respected people from the outside. We prayed and studied New Testament passages together. We traveled out of state to a conference. We took a short retreat. We looked at churches that had clarity in their calling and were impacting their world.

I'll be honest with you. It's scary for a leader to bring other people into the process. But there is nothing more exciting than being with a group of people and seeing the synergy grow as thoughts and ideas crystallize, knowing that all these people are on board and sense God speaking. It's an awesome experience!

Be Faithful Today

On the day Paul was converted on the Damascus Road, God shined a light and transformed Paul's life. But the Lord did not tell him immediately what his calling was. The Lord only said, "Now get up and go into the city, and you will be told what you must do" (Acts 9:6). God was testing Paul to see if he would be obedient.

The Lord then spoke to another person named Ananias and told him that Paul was coming and would be a chosen instrument to proclaim the gospel to the Gentiles (Acts 9:15). I find it interesting that God told Ananias that Paul would be ministering to the Gentiles before He told Paul. God was giving Paul what he needed, when he needed it. As Paul obeyed and followed, God made his calling evident.

What are you supposed to do today? Just do it. The best you can—do it. Don't miss today because you don't know what God wants you to do tomorrow. He may be testing you. Preparing you. Molding you.

Throw Out Some Fleeces

Early in my walk with Christ, I knew God had a specific calling for my life, and at one point, I thought I was going to be a missionary. I even went to

Bible College with that purpose in mind. But the following summer I took my first foreign mission trip. It was a tremendous experience. I wanted to go back. I also knew without a doubt—100% positive—that God was *not* calling me to be a full-time missionary.

Sometimes we need to try some things. Get in the game and see what God is blessing. The saying is true enough that it's worth repeating: "It's always easier to steer a car when it's moving."

Start Here

When an existing church is ready to address the issue of culture, the first step is to wrestle with God and seek a clear sense of calling. When you know what God is asking your church to do and be, you will usually find that your core values begin to fall naturally into place. Without a calling, though, you may end up settling for values that are incongruent or counterproductive to the long-term potential of your church.

For example, I was recently consulting with a congregation that has been struggling for a number of years. This church is a sleeping giant, and the leaders have been seeking the Lord and asking God for direction. After going through many of the steps in this chapter, they finally came to see what they believed God was calling them to do and be. The board was unified. The staff was energized. Yet they knew that a percentage of longtime members would not be supportive because they were not open to anything new and usually wanted to maintain status quo, even though the church was hemorrhaging.

Traditionally, this congregation had placed a high emphasis on the value of "unity." On one hand, this sounds noble. But some longtime members had developed a sense of entitlement and were more concerned with their wants and needs than the overall health of the church. Whenever the leadership suggested any kind of change, this group of people would make a stir and talk about how change was causing disunity. They were using unity as a way to control the agenda. In the past, the leadership had a history of backing down whenever people complained. Their default was to pacify more than to lead, even when they felt God was directing them. Part of the reason the church was struggling was because the leadership would pull in the reins in order to keep the peace whenever anyone was upset.

Now that the church board members had a sense of calling, they were able to prayerfully establish intentional values, which helped to forge a culture that would enable them to make their calling a reality. They were also able to de-emphasize other values that were hindering the congregation. They still wanted unity in the church, but their commitment to their calling was greater than the need to pacify chronic complainers. The calling of their church and their intentional values began to trump individual agendas.

This is why you start with the process of discerning God's calling. Once you discern this, you can begin to determine the actual and aspirational values that will help shape the culture of the church in order to live out that calling. Without a clear and comprehensive calling, there is often a lack of symmetry, and you may settle for biblical values that become self-limiting.

Chapter 11

TESTING THE SOIL

"Facts are friends."

Soil is a complex mixture that varies in texture, pH level, and nutrients. The quality of the soil predetermines its effectiveness and potential. Therefore, it is common for farmers, gardeners, or anyone else working the ground to occasionally take a soil analysis. A soil analysis is a test that determines the specific content of the soil, revealing its strengths and deficiencies.

To take these tests, the analyst collects a sample from the selected ground by digging down and pulling up some dirt. He will then put the dirt sample in a bag and move to another part of the same area and repeat the process. After he has gotten several individual samples, he mixes the samples together and has them evaluated. This reveals the specific makeup of that ground, allowing the analyst to determine its quality.

Leaders need to do the same thing. There are ways you can analyze the culture of your church—ways you can bore down and see what's at work beneath the surface. Unlike working with real soil, there are no specific tests that will give you an exact read on your congregation, but if you take multiple samples and then process them, you are likely to get an indication of what you've got and what you might need to do in order to boost the quality of your soil.

The following suggestions are more of a compass to give you direction than a roadmap to show you a definite path. You should not feel the need to act on every suggestion listed in this chapter. Apply only the aspects that you feel will help you uncover the culture of *your* church, and then move on.

Dig in Various Places

It's very important that you tap into a diverse number of people when evaluating church culture. It is tempting to believe you've already got an effective read on your congregation or to take only a small and narrow sample. But the results are only as good as the samples taken. So, if you don't tap into large enough groups of people, you will get unreliable results. Here are some of the groups you'll need to engage.

Church Leaders

The leaders are the influencers in the church, or at least they are representatives who are acting on behalf of the influencers. And if you are ever going to enhance the culture of your congregation, you will need to have a critical mass of your leaders on board. Therefore, you need to start by evaluating the personalities, beliefs, convictions, and spiritual health of the leadership. Are your board members passive or active? Do they lead or micromanage? Are they bureaucratic or empowering? Do they represent a cross section of the church or just a subset? Do they live in the past or look to the future? What kind of issues are they united on, and where are they divided? Is there a lot of turnover? Do they understand the mindsets of people outside the church or just those inside the church?

Then you must look at your staff and lay leaders. Is there continuity? Are they working together as a team or just as individuals? What issues or beliefs are they unified on? What are the strengths and weakness of individual staff members? What kind of skills do they have? What are their passions? Do they love the Lord, or are they just doing a job? Do they have individual agendas and convictions? Are there any holes or obvious gaps in the staffing that is limiting the church?

You need to start by assessing the leadership. If you're divided at the top, you'll be divided at the bottom. If you don't have buy-in, unity, or direction at the leadership level, it is going to be almost impossible to redirect the ship. The only way you can work toward a healthy culture is to understand what you're working with among your leaders.

The Congregation

After you've evaluated the leadership, you then need to address the church as a whole. This doesn't mean that every single person needs to participate, but you do need to connect with various groups of people, giving as many as you can an opportunity to engage. This not only gives you good information, but it also gives people ownership of the process. If people are engaged and have input into the process, they are more likely to have buy-in to the possible solutions. Here are some suggestions for going about this.

Use a formal survey that is outsourced or purchased to engage the congregation. You can find consultants or organizations that already have surveys put together. Talking to other church leaders or a simple Google search can connect you with some of these. If you decide to go this route, be sure you select a survey that will help you uncover mindsets and values, not just personal preferences.

You can also develop your own survey based upon your own set of questions.[25] This is a little more work on the front end, but sometimes it is more beneficial. You can put together a written survey that people can fill out, or you can do something online. Online surveys are easy to set up, and they will provide you all the answers printed out. Just make sure your survey is not too long. Fewer questions that are well constructed are always better.

Another option is to put together focus groups by gathering people together and giving them a prepared set of questions to discuss. Focus groups can be extremely helpful because they are conversationally based, which allows for a deeper probing of issues and a wider range of questions. But I would suggest you have someone from the outside come in to lead these discussions if you go this route. People tend to be more honest talking to someone from outside the church. And outside facilitators are going to be more objective as they lead the meeting and summarize the responses.

Visitors

Getting visitor feedback is another way to gather soil samples. Many struggling churches identify a primary strength of their congregations as "friendly." This is especially true with smaller churches. Whenever I hear this response, I ask this follow-up question: "Is that what visitors say?" The reason I ask this is because people on the inside almost always have a different experience than people who are guests. I can't tell you how many times church leaders have told me their church is friendly, but when I ask the follow-up question, they admit visitors have told them their church is unfriendly or cliquish. Therefore, you need some form of an exit interview with your guests in order to understand what they see, feel, and experience.

Once you get feedback from your visitors, listen to what they say. Don't be defensive. Listen and learn.

You can do exit interviews with visitors in a variety of ways. You can send them cards in the mail or e-mail them. You can give them follow-up phone calls. Or, if your church has enough visitor flow, you can set up a dinner or focus group meeting for new people who are just starting to attend.

Don't make this too complicated or drawn out. Just ask visitors some simple, open-ended questions such as these: What brought you here? What brought you back? What were your first impressions? What did you like? Was there anything that made you uncomfortable? Do you have any suggestions for us that might help us better connect with visitors in the future?

Outside Eyes

On top of this, it's important to bring in people with wisdom and an unbiased opinion to speak into your ministry. One day I invited an experienced pastor named Jerry Harris to visit our church. I began giving Jerry a tour of our building, and we weren't five minutes into our time together when he said bluntly, "Your building is killing you." Then he gave me several specific things he saw to back up his statement. We knew that our building limited us, but Jerry's words gave us a sense of urgency and opened our eyes to some blind spots. His comments helped us define the reality of our situation.

Sure enough, our church began to cap out in the upcoming months as our facilities became an obvious bottleneck. Jerry's insights proved to be spot on and reminded us of the value in inviting wise, seasoned people to bring a fresh perspective to situations.

The bottom line is you need to step outside of your own bubble, and you must talk with your leaders, the congregation, visitors, and outside advisors. Ask lots of questions, and ask good questions. I have included an extended list of questions you might want to address in Appendix II. Once you tap into the right groups of people and ask the right questions, you must listen well and reflect upon what you are hearing. This information gathering process is the first step in evaluating the culture of your church.

Double-Loop Learning

As you gather information, you must know that simply identifying the obvious issues is not enough to understand the soil makeup of your church. But too often this is where church leaders stop.

I was once visiting with the leaders of a struggling church where the congregation was getting noticeably older and attendance was on a sharp decline. They asked me a number of questions about methodology and how to connect with the younger generations. They were looking for programmatic solutions to turn the church around.

Rather than give them answers, I began to question them about the culture of their church. In doing so, I discovered a lack of unity in the board concerning philosophies of leadership. There were also no clear boundaries or expectations for board members. I found a democratic mindset among the congregation. They felt that everything should be voted on and that board members were basically representatives of the people. I also uncovered an inability for many members to discern the difference between issues of taste and truth. To make matters worse, there was also a noticeable lack of trust between staff and board members. In other words, the problems facing this congregation were much deeper than just style and programs. Changing the methods of ministry was not going to do anything lasting because there were much deeper issues beneath the surface. The people involved were nice, and they all appeared sincere. But there were multiple levels of dysfunction, and they didn't even realize it.

The way many churches function when they are struggling is to look for new programs or more efficient methods to get better results (see Chapter 2). This is known as single-loop learning. It involves looking at the obvious with the end goal of trying to do something different in order to get better results.

Single-loop learning asks questions like these: "What are we doing, and how can we do it differently to get better results?" Or, "What are we not doing that we need to start doing in order to get better results?" But in churches with an unhealthy culture this rarely works, and the members are often left more frustrated than before. The reason is that they are unaware or unwilling to address the deeper issues.

On the other hand, double-loop learning looks at the surface, then circles back around and asks a completely different set of questions, such as, "Why are we even doing this in the first place? What is driving us to do this, and does it need to be done?" Double-loop learning understands that there are deeper issues, which need to be addressed. Therefore, it moves beyond the basic focus of action and results, and it probes into the variables and assumptions that are at work behind the scenes.

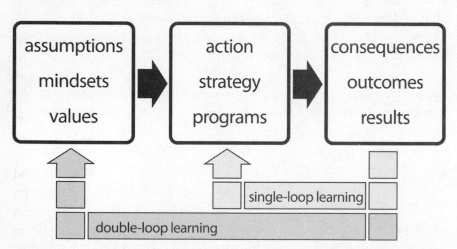

To understand the difference between single-loop and double-loop learning, consider what your church might do if the building was too hot or too cold.

Single-loop learning comes up with a predictable solution, such as turning the thermostat up or down and adjusting the temperature setting to get it comfortable. Simple enough, right? But double-loop learning will look for issues beyond the obvious. For example, is the room properly insulated? Do the units need to be serviced for better efficiency? Are the vents and thermostat properly positioned? Should there be a set of expectations communicated for dress at certain times of the year?

Double-loop learning does not just settle for the quickest and easiest answers. It looks at the assumptions behind the issue and seeks to determine if there are other variables at work. Double-loop learning often exposes root problems that superficial solutions will never address.

To understand the culture of your church and the values that drive it, you must think in ways that are consistent with double-loop learning. You need to wrestle with the mindsets and assumptions that are at work behind the scenes. Often what we perceive as long-term solutions are not the best or healthiest ones. We need to go deeper and look for the issues beneath the issues.

Process the Samples

Once you've sampled the culture and reflected on what you've learned, you need to collate and process what you've discovered. The best way to do this is in the context of a team. Ideally, this will be some form of your church leadership, including board and/or staff members. The main thing is to include people who want to be involved and are going to help you move things forward. If at all possible, you need to avoid obstinate and critical people. You don't need naysayers to be part of this phase.

Once you've got your team in place, take several evenings in a compact period of time to work together. Stretching it out with long gaps between meetings tends to break momentum and causes a loss of synergy. Sometimes the process may take months to complete, but you need to have focused concentration to properly evaluate and discuss the information.

Better yet, take an overnight retreat somewhere to get started or to wrap it up. Get a cabin. Go to a church camp. Check into a hotel. Just get away from your normal environment and spend focused time working through the process. If you can get an outside facilitator, consultant, or another seasoned pastor to guide your time, even better.

When it's time to actually do the work of processing and determining how to move forward, a four-part outline will help you do so. This can be done in a SWAP review.[26] The SWAP review allows you to have group discussions based upon the information you've gathered and to draw some non-threatening conclusions and funnel them down to clear and viable action points. This is what it looks like:

Strengths

Make a list of your congregation's strengths. This includes what you are doing well and the areas God appears to be blessing. Also list where you have traction or momentum and the ministries that are bearing fruit. Include the healthy values you already have in place and the opportunities you have that can be leveraged and built upon.

Weaknesses

You then need to list the areas where your church is struggling. What obstacles are you facing? What challenges are looming ahead? What is not working? Are there blind spots you've been avoiding? Where do you have value gaps— unhealthy values that are hindering you or healthy values that are absent? Which things need to be addressed immediately, and what things can wait?

Applications

You must then move beyond theory and discussion, putting down on paper what you are going to do in light of the information you have gathered, prayed over, and discussed. You will begin to list specific action points that need to be addressed. Don't make your list too long. If it is long, prioritize and break it down into time frames. It's also helpful to determine who is responsible for what applications and then to talk about how you are going to follow-up down the road.

Principles

You are now at the point of actually determining the values for your congregation. More than just making a list of applications that deal with programs, ministries, people, or policies, you must define and establish a list of values that need to be cultivated within the church. Your list should include existing values that need to be reinforced, expanded, or built upon. You also might need to consciously eliminate, tweak, or move away from some values that are presently part of the church's culture. You will need to determine if there are any new values the church should aspire to, which can be cultivated over time. Put together your list of principles (values), and whittle it down to between four and seven.

After finalizing your list of values, you need to define exactly what those values mean and look like within your church. This will include a definition, scripture verses, and maybe even practical examples of your values in action. Don't just assume people will have the same understanding you do of the values you list.

Now that you have sampled the soil, reflected on its composition, and processed the results by walking through the SWAP principle, you are ready to begin instilling your values into the life of the church.

Chapter 12

BREAKING GROUND

"Change is inevitable. Growth is intentional." – Glenda Cloud

John Evans is a master gardener from Alaska who loves to grow vegetables—not just any vegetables, but giant ones. He has multiple world records, including a nineteen-pound carrot and a forty-five-pound head of cabbage. When asked to name the key to his success, Evans said, "The secret is in the soil."

Understanding the importance of soil quality, he intentionally does things to prepare the ground and maximize its potential. For example, he makes his own fertilizer that is referred to as "tea." He takes compost, bacteria, and other nutrients, then cooks them into a dark brown, brew-like formula. He uses this to boost the health and productivity of the soil.

John Evans doesn't just plant the seeds and passively leave the rest to chance. He realizes that if he wants to maximize the plant's potential, he needs to take the initiative. He knows there are things he can do to enhance the quality of the soil, so he acts intentionally and puts his knowledge into action.

This is relevant to us because a church can develop a wonderful set of values on paper, yet at some point actions speak louder than words. The church must move beyond theory and good intentions and start to act in accordance with what they advocate. This chapter identifies nine principles that are key in making the values of your church an influential factor in shaping its culture.

Utilize the Pound Principle

In marketing circles, there is a saying, "It takes seven to stick." This means people have to receive a message multiple times before it begins to settle in. Generally, that number is a minimum of seven. The first time people encounter a message they don't usually hear it. Even if they hear it, they don't receive it. Even if they receive it, they often reject it. Even if they accept it, they usually forget it. We must send the same message multiple times in multiple ways before that message sticks.

Dave Jacobs, a friend of mine who coaches pastors, posted a blog that addressed what he calls the "Pound Principle."[27] Here's what he says:

> Anything worth saying is worth pounding. The values you hold are worth saying. If you want to effectively communicate your values, then you will need to repeat them over and over, pounding them into the minds of your people. Notice I said, "effectively communicate?" Effective communication results in comprehension and action. I can preach a sermon, but that's no guarantee my congregation will comprehend (understand) or apply (take action upon) my words. I must not assume communication is occurring just because words are flowing. Certain things enhance communication.

> One communication skill is that of repetition. Repetition ensures communication. Whatever your values are, those things you want your people to walk in, those principles will need to be hammered/pounded, repeated, and reinforced again and again and again. For example, if you want your people to be "givers," it won't be enough to preach on giving once a year. We won't produce people who "share their faith" as a result of one great sermon on personal evangelism. Repetition ensures communication.

You are trying to create a certain kind of church. This
"kind of church" is based on your values. If it's important
enough to be a value, then it's important enough to bear
repeating. People learn through repetition. Communication
is enhanced through repetition. What values do your people
need hammered into them over the next twelve months?
Develop a plan and start pounding.

One great sermon...
   One good meeting...
      One nice article is never enough.

You have to consistently send the message. The more creative and the more
mediums you use, the more likely the message will be remembered. Here
are three basic modes that you should leverage when communicating your
values.

Verbal

Using the spoken word to communicate your values is the most obvious form
of communication, especially for church leaders. It's preaching individual
sermons and series. It's teaching in classes, groups, and Bible studies. It's
sharing stories and using testimonies. It's recording video messages and v-logs.
It's strategically using the mission banquet and the congregational meeting to
say something valuable rather than just the same old, same old.

Written

Take the same message you are preaching and teaching and communicate it
through written forms. Preachers often make the mistake of thinking they
have to come up with something fresh every time, but wise teachers know they
can and should communicate a valuable message multiple times, in multiple
ways, and in multiple forms. Take your messages and summarize or repost
them in written form. Put something in the bulletin, newsletter, a brochure,
or on the webpage. Set up a blog. Send out a special letter that is written from
the heart. Use social media. Don't just speak the message: put it in writing.

Visual

When we defined the vision statement for our church a few years back, one of the more artistic members of our team said, "Why are we just talking about this? Why don't we develop some graphics or artwork to illustrate what we're sharing? Images capture my attention more than just words." He was right. As a result, we developed five images, one for each aspect of our vision, and we made posters that we put in the sanctuary of our fixed campus.

You will really help yourself if you can develop graphics, pictures, posters, videos, or artwork to illustrate and communicate what you're speaking and writing.

Effective visual communication should include making sure your physical environment reflects the values you espouse. For example, it is tough to emphasize community as a core value if you've got a sanctuary that is long, narrow, bland, and filled with wooden pews. If the people are sitting on hard, uncomfortable seats twenty rows away from the stage and looking at nothing but the backs of heads, their experience doesn't communicate that relationships are important. Such environments usually feel sterile and impersonal. On the other hand, warmer colors, softer seating, strategic lighting, and seating patterns that allow for eye contact and easier communication enhance the possibility of people connecting and experiencing some measure of community.

When you know what you want to communicate, you must have a consistent message that is creatively sent across all three of these mediums. If you do so, the chance of you being heard improves significantly.

Communicate Wisely

As you communicate in various ways, there are also some important things you can do to help people intellectually buy in to what you are saying. Here are three teaching tips that will enhance the values you are trying to instill:

Sell the Problem

Don't just communicate your values; let people know the reasons behind them and why those reasons are important. In the book *Transformational Church,* the authors say, "Churches do not change until the pain of staying the same is greater than the pain of changing."[28] If there is no pain, there is no urgency and no burden felt by the members. You have to help people see and feel the need. Point them toward a preferable future, and show them the predictable consequences of staying the same.

Right before I came to Richwoods, the people in leadership were having serious conversations about whether they would be able to keep the church open or not. The core members were beginning to realize that if they didn't do something different, the church was going to die. When I came, I reminded them of this and talked about where the church was naturally headed if things stayed the same. I asked the question, "Where are our kids and grandkids?" I shared statistics and told stories. I wasn't trying to browbeat them; I was trying to define reality and remind them of why we needed to change.

This is what is often referred to as sowing seeds of discontent—intentionally doing things to highlight a problem and allowing people to feel the pain before jumping to solutions. It's been said that people don't change until they hurt enough that they have to, learn enough that they are able to, or see enough that they want to. We have to sell the problem, not just the values.

Connect with the Past

When I talked with longtime members at my church, I quickly began to hear some common stories about their passion for missions and how the church was giving over 30% of its budget to this ministry. They had done several short-term mission trips and even commissioned members of the church to full-time foreign missionary service. This was part of the church's heritage, and it was where they found their identity as a congregation.

Rather than ignoring or downplaying this passion, I tried to highlight and celebrate it. I commended the people on their commitment to missions and their compassion for lost people. Then I challenged them. I told them our church was outstanding at foreign missions, but we weren't doing anything to reach our own community. Our Jerusalem was being neglected at the expense of the "uttermost parts of the world." I took something positive and tried to expand it, enhance it, and redefine it.

Sometimes leaders can fall into the temptation of shaming their people, running them down, and diminishing yesterday. I think it's better to encourage and give honor where honor is due. By celebrating the positives of the past, it is easier to direct people's attention to the future and challenge them to build on whatever good they've already done.

Teach While You Teach

When you teach values, you need to find ways to teach them indirectly. For example, if one of the values you need to instill is outreach and evangelism, you can always do a sermon series, and that will touch many people. That's a direct way of handling the subject and is appropriate. However, some might avoid church because they don't want to be challenged in this area. Some will be out of town and miss most of the series. Others will be present, but will tune you out because they've heard it before and aren't interested. Furthermore, once you've done the series, you likely won't be doing another on this subject for a year or more. And what about the new people who started to attend church after the series? Now you've fired your bullet, but it's going to be a while before you can reload.

On the other hand, let's say that you are doing a series on trusting God, and you give an illustration on sharing your faith. The sermon is about trust, but you're weaving one of your core values into it. People don't expect it. Their guard is down. You've just tied one of your key principles to a practical element of the faith. The next month you do a series on prayer and you designate one point of one message to praying for lost friends and family. In both cases, you are intentionally teaching the church the value of outreach, but you're doing so indirectly.

The consistent routine of finding ways to weave core values into the life of the church is invaluable. You are making it practical. You are reinforcing what you've already taught. And you are sending a consistent message across a number of different topics, which communicates to the people that this is a key principle for the church and a relevant part of their lives.

Leverage MCs

Another important resource to tap into is what I call MCs. This is a term I use to describe four types of people who influence the culture of a church from outside the church. Each has a slightly different purpose, but they all bring credibility and freshness when it comes to addressing the local congregation. These people are seen as objective and are usually perceived as being experts in some form. The fact that they usually come with credentials and expertise means their words carry weight. The four influencers I refer to as MCs are models, mentors, coaches, and consultants. While there is some overlap, here is a breakdown of each.

Models

Models are people and churches we look up to as examples to follow (1 Corinthians 11:1). That doesn't mean we should duplicate everything they are doing. It just means we observe and learn from them. There is a theological and/or philosophical connection that makes part or all of their ministries attractive and relevant. Therefore, models exemplify ways that we want our church to look, feel, and act.

Mentors

Mentors are individuals who pour into us directly. They are not only modeling but also teaching us. They are ahead of us in their knowledge, experience, and insight. Out of their overflow, they share practical and spiritual insights in order to help us grow and develop. Mentors can be people we personally know, or they can be people we've never met but follow at a distance by listening, reading, and observing.

Coaches

Coaches also have wisdom and experience beyond our own but differ slightly from mentors because they are developing us in a one-on-one relationship that revolves around our specific needs. Mentors usually start with what they have on their hearts to share, but coaches usually start with the specific needs of the people they are helping. There is almost always some form of a personal relationship with a coach.

Consultants

Consultants are seasoned professionals who come in to address isolated challenges facing the church. They evaluate, troubleshoot, and then make recommendations for what the church needs to do in order to move forward. Consultants almost always cost money, and the church is one of several clients. The relationship between the church and the consultant is almost always more professional than personal.

To illustrate the difference between MCs, let me use golf as an example. First of all, there are certain professional golfers I look up to as examples. Perhaps it's their character, their witness for Christ, the way they conduct themselves on the course, or something about how they play the game. But out of the hundreds of professional golfers, there are only a few I respect and follow closely. They can inspire me, encourage me, and offer some value to me as a Christian and casual golfer. These would be models.

I also have friends who are good golfers. I don't take lessons from them, but when we play, I ask questions, listen, and pick up random insights. In addition, I follow a couple of authors who write teaching books about golf. If I'm looking for tips on putting, driving, etc., these authors are the first ones I look to, and I am very familiar with them. These could be considered mentors because, out of their skill and wisdom, they have a direct influence on my golf game.

When I actually sign up for golf lessons, a golf coach instructs me. One hour per week for the better part of one summer, the golf coach observes my swing, points out my weaknesses, shows me how to correct them, and gives me specific things to practice between sessions. He works with me individually and walks through various aspects of my swing. He helps me break bad habits, such as releasing my wrists too quickly and coming outside the ball with my irons. I wouldn't call him a model, but he is much more than a mentor: he is a coach.

Finally, let's say that my game is at a plateau. I just can't break through to the next level. So, assuming that I've got an extra ten thousand dollars, I decide to travel to Florida and have a personal consultation with a top-notch PGA coach like Butch Harmon. I meet with him for a couple of hours, and he gives me direction on how I can improve my game. I then come back home and work to implement the changes, perhaps even asking my coach and mentors to help me apply what the consultant has shown me.

While there is some overlap, each of the MCs has value and plays a slightly different role in helping develop and mature my golf game. They give me objective input, fresh perspectives, and new information.

The same thing is true when it comes to leading a church and influencing culture. MCs give us confidence and accelerate the learning curve. They are able to stretch, encourage, point out blind spots, expose us to new information and resources, and equip the congregation in ways that may be hard for us to do on the inside.

I once brought in a consultant to talk with our elders about church governance. He did more in ninety minutes to chart a new direction for the leadership of our church than I was able to do in a year. I could give multiple examples of how MCs have positively influenced my church and me, but I'll simply say this: please take advantage of them. Even if you can't afford to bring someone on site, you can read blogs, meet up with other pastors, sign up for online coaching, subscribe to podcasts or video messages, or even read books with your leaders.[29] Ultimately though, you shouldn't try to change the culture of your church alone.

Invest in New Blood

Another way we pull the congregation forward is by connecting with new people. And I'm not just talking about being friendly; I'm talking about trying to invest in the new attendees coming into your church. These people are going to buy in more quickly, and they tend to have a different perspective of the leadership than the longtime stakeholders. Longtime members can have an entitlement attitude, whereas newcomers tend to be more supportive and respectful of the leadership. New people help bring about a tipping point, where the culture of the church suddenly changes and a majority of the people are embodying the values of the congregation. Without attracting and assimilating new people, reaching this tipping point is very difficult.

If you are fortunate enough to attract newcomers, it is essential that you have some formal training mechanism to help explain the culture of the church to them. Defining the culture up front is a bit risky because it has the potential of pushing some people away, even though it will attract others. It is a risk that must be taken, however. The last thing you want to do is to attract someone to your church with his or her own agenda or a false belief about who you are and where you're going. By defining your beliefs, your calling, and your values early on, you remove ambiguity. If you are slow to define these things, or if you never do, you open the door for immature believers and people with agendas to infiltrate your church and do more harm than good. If you don't define your culture, they may.

Our church offers a newcomers' class about every eight weeks. We push this class hard, and when people arrive, we don't water it down. We welcome them, have some fun, do some interactive things, and then define who we are as a church and where we believe God wants us to go. At one of these classes, a man became upset because he didn't like some of the things I was sharing about our church's calling. I explained, "The agenda of our church is not up for grabs. If you don't like what I'm saying, that's fine, but the reason we do this is so that you can determine if this is the right church for you or not. If you don't agree, I would rather have you discover that now and find a church that is more to your liking than to have you continue to attend here with the false belief that we're going to be something we're not." This man didn't like it. He left the class and never came back. A short time later I was talking to the pastor of a church the man had previously attended. The pastor wanted to warn me that the individual was a defiant troublemaker who bounced to a new church every couple of years. I can't tell you how glad I am that he left before he got involved. The main reason he left so quickly was because we were intentional about defining our culture up front.

The flip side of this is that almost all of the other people in that class stayed. They were energized, dialed in, and excited to be a part of our congregation. When you connect with new blood, the learning curve is short, and the ownership is high. New people, combined with your committed core, are the ones who spread the church's values like dye in water.

Enable Reverse Flow

Another way to influence culture is by what I call "reverse flow." On a cruise to Alaska, I had the privilege of taking an excursion and seeing a river with a small set of rapids that actually flowed both ways. Its current flowed downhill into the ocean, but due to the slight grade, when the tide would rise, it would actually push water backwards a significant distance. One part of the day the river flowed one way. Another part of the day it flowed the other.

I share this because another mistake we can make is to focus all our attention on communicating to our people while never giving them the opportunity to reverse the flow. I've read that communication occurs four times faster from the top down than from the bottom up. It's much easier for the leadership to share what they want the people to hear than it is for the people to be heard by the leadership.

If people feel heard, they are much more likely to stay connected and on board. Furthermore, they may actually provide valuable insights that the leadership needs to hear. Even if they are complaining or making suggestions that are not going to work, they are more likely to stay in the game if they feel heard.

Therefore, it's important to set up channels of communication so that feedback, frustration, and input can flow upstream. And when people take advantage of these opportunities, it's imperative that the leaders are not defensive. Bite your tongue. Ask questions. But don't argue in the real time. Tell them you'll think about it, sleep on it, or talk about it with the other leaders. Then follow up with them and have a conversation. This kind of open communication may produce a few headaches, but giving people permission to offer input ultimately builds trust. And you may learn something valuable. The flip side of this is that if people don't *feel* heard, they will internalize their frustrations and at some point blow up or walk away.

Hold People Accountable

The book of Galatians records another quick but powerful lesson on how to change culture. The story occurs in chapter two, where the apostle Paul confronts Peter for his hypocrisy in dealing with the Gentiles. Paul wrote, "When Cephas came to Antioch, I opposed him to his face, because he stood condemned" (2:11). Peter struggled with the acceptance of Gentiles when he was in the presence of more conservative Jewish leaders. When Paul encountered Peter's hypocrisy, he didn't just go home and tell his family, nor did he call his friends on the phone and vent; instead, Paul confronted the issue. He addressed Peter to his face and in the presence of other people (vs. 14).

There are some strong personalities that have little problem with confrontation, but far more common in the church is a passivity and unwillingness to address people and problems head on. One of the unspoken, yet rampant, sins in many congregations is passive-aggressive behavior. This is the unwillingness to confront people in honest face-to-face dialogue while attacking them behind their backs through gossip, slander, manipulation, or personal attacks.

I cannot emphasize strongly enough how important it is that we lovingly challenge people and confront behavior that is incongruent with the values of the church. When people see that they are going to be held accountable, they will run, yield and grow, or engage in a showdown. But sometimes that's what it takes. One thing is for sure: you are not helping them, or the church as a whole, by enabling sinful behavior and allowing immaturity to reign. I don't care how long someone has attended the church or what their title is; you must hold people accountable for inappropriate attitudes and behavior. You don't have to be a jerk, even though you may be labeled as one, but you can't succumb to passivity. It is not biblical to avoid conflict. And it's not helpful.

I hate interpersonal conflict, and I don't like confrontation, but I cannot think of one instance where I've confronted someone for sinful or inappropriate behavior and regretted it. As a matter of fact, the only regrets I have are from not addressing people when I should have. When you begin to graciously hold people accountable for their actions and their words, you are on your way to establishing a healthy culture.

Celebrate Success

When you see people living out the church's values, give them a word of encouragement. Tell other people. Have them give a testimony. Celebrate and make positive examples out of them. Too often we want to preach against what needs to be changed more than praising what is being done right. Most people in the church want encouragement, and they want to please God. By recognizing good behavior and acknowledging it, you are motivating people to move in the direction they need to go. Not only that, you are also giving the congregation real life examples of what it means to live out the values of the church.

Show the Way

Values are caught as much as taught. They are most infectious when people can see them genuinely embodied in the lives of people around them. You can duplicate programs, but you can't duplicate values. They must be incarnate. They need to be owned and lived out, especially by the leaders, before they settle into the hearts of the larger church body.

One of the names given to Jesus was the Great Shepherd. He came not in the mold of a dominant CEO, but as a servant leader. A shepherd gives the image of one who leads, not by walking behind and driving the sheep, but by being in front of them. When Jesus called His disciples, He didn't just tell them what to do; He called them to *follow* Him. Even the Apostle Paul exhorted the Corinthians to follow his example as he followed Christ (1 Corinthians 11:1).

In order to shape values, we must model them by leading in such a way that others catch the wake and follow. One thing is for sure: people will never own values they don't see their leaders living out.

On the other hand, values begin to go viral when groups of people begin to own and live them. When this happens, things spread to the fringes. People who are not a part of the inner circle may now see, hear, or come in contact with others on the edges who are embodying the values of the church. This expands the influence, and it reinforces what's important.

Walk with the People

I once worked with a church that had been the same size for a long time. The church faced some of the classic and predictable obstacles consistent with congregations that plateau at that size. When the pastor left the church, the leaders were determined to get a minister who had experience working in a larger congregation, in the hope that the new pastor could help lead them into new territory.

After a while they found their guy. He was young, talented, and passionate, and he had worked in a large congregation. Everyone was excited and ready to go when he started. But this young man made a huge mistake that ultimately led to a short tenure at this church. He didn't understand the importance of relationships.

For all the weaknesses of the previous pastor, one of his greatest strengths was that he was a wonderful shepherd. He cared for the people, and they knew it. But when the new pastor came in, he immediately began to lead this church as if he were the pastor of a megachurch. He instructed the secretary that he would not see people without an appointment. He worked with his door closed and rarely had time for hospital visits. And, even though the church only had a few staff members, he insisted on communicating with memos and emails rather than walking down the hall and talking face-to-face. He was either too foolish or too afraid to actually connect with people on a personal basis. Needless to say, he didn't last very long.

Changing the culture of an existing church is an emotional pursuit for the people involved, and part of the way you navigate this is through relationships. You must authentically invest in people if you are going to influence them. People want to believe you care not just for God, but also for the church and for them as individuals.

Relationships are at the core of the New Testament. Jesus summarized obedience in two commands—love God and love people. When He sent out the disciples for the first time, He didn't send them as individuals. He sent them out in pairs. And in the book of Acts, we don't read about any lone rangers. We read, instead, about teams and groups of people who take the gospel from Jerusalem to Judea, to Samaria, and then to the uttermost parts of the world.

In addition, almost all of the Epistles have heavy relational components. They include direct teachings, greetings, salutations, and words of encouragement. They use phrases like "brothers and sisters," "my dear children," "my true son," "friend," "companion," and "fellow workers." They talk about households, holy kisses, and hospitality. They challenge people to love, forgive, and walk in unity. Over 50 times we read exhortations associated with the phrase "one another."

The New Testament is all about relationships, yet it's easy for us to reduce the church to titles, positions, and impersonal truth. We can be tempted to flex our muscles and tell people what they are supposed to do and believe, rather than walking alongside them.

Without emphasizing relationships, we are missing a key component of the New Testament, and we are limiting our ability to influence culture. Trying to instill new values and getting people to think differently are not just intellectual exercises; they are emotional investments. Many times, people resist because they are scared or they don't grasp why change is necessary. Furthermore, studies show that over 75% of adults are middle or later adopters. This means they are hesitant to embrace new ideas. Their personality and nature are resistant to and skeptical of the new. It takes time for most people to process and buy in, but when people have relationships with others they trust, they are more likely to get on board even when they are unsure. The reason: *relationships almost always trump information*.

Carl George once spoke about the importance of leading the church from a position of influence rather than from a title.[30] He noted that founding pastors of a church have built-in authority and that people in the church generally follow them without much concern. Yet when a pastor goes to an existing congregation, there are various dynamics at work that make it much harder to lead and direct the congregation. It becomes important for the pastor to earn credibility and, therefore, to be granted the permission to lead. George then says that the best way to earn trust is to love the people and to be true to your values:

> As a pastoral leader you must differentiate yourself from your congregation. The way you differentiate is by articulating your values and goals. If they are derived from Christ, are biblically based, and if they proceed from your values, sooner or later they will accept your headship.
>
> But the key in this process is that just as a head must stay connected to the body, you must stay connected to the people. Even in the face of reluctance, pushback, criticism, and even slander, you must stay connected to the people.
>
> You do this by remaining patient, loving, and kind, even through periods of resistance. When the people see that the pastor truly cares for them and has their best interest at heart, they usually come to respect him as a person. Once they respect him, they are then likely to embrace the pastor's views, values, and goals. But you must stay connected with the people emotionally and by modeling lots of love. When you do this, headship becomes leadership.

In other words, the people of an existing congregation follow and give the pastor permission to lead not because of a title, but out of respect for who the pastor is and because they believe he sincerely cares for them. It takes persistence, prayer, and lots of grace because it takes time to gain permission. But once you have it, your values are respected, and they become contagious.

Do Something

Once you know what values are essential to shaping the culture of your church, you must intentionally break ground and work to impress these values upon the congregation. This is challenging and often draining. It's not easy, nor is it a quick turnaround—it's a long-term investment. Yet it's one that must be made.

Don't think for a minute that good intentions are enough or that you'll get lucky and things will just fall into place. Hope is not a strategy. You may get fortunate, but it's unlikely. If you want God to bear fruit through your ministry, you must cultivate a healthy environment for that to happen. You've got to address the soil and purposely do things to enhance its quality. You must be intentional. You must act!

FINAL THOUGHTS

*"I have done what was mine to do; now you must
do what is yours to do."* – St. Francis

The summer of 2012 was one of the hottest on record in American history. Across most of the Midwest, the heat was combined with a severe drought that caused many farmers to see below average yields. Some farmers just mowed their fields and called their insurance agent because the crops were so poor it wasn't even worth the time and money to harvest. The following winter, California had a cold snap where temperatures dipped into the 20s. Citrus farmers were scrambling to cover fruit trees. A deep or prolonged frost could stunt the growth of the fruit and even destroy the entire harvest.

So, even if a farmer has the best soil available, there are other factors that come into play: too much rain, not enough rain, damaging insects, unexpected frosts, windstorms, tornadoes, or ill-timed planting. All of these things can negatively influence potential outcomes in spite of soil quality.

The same is true in the church.

While I have emphasized the importance of culture as a key element for a healthy, vibrant, and effective ministry, I must also remind you that there are other factors at work. You can cultivate healthy values in a church and still find that it's a grind with little visible fruit appearing. The external environment of the community, an affair inside the church, one contentious or stubborn board member, a rogue staff member, or a severe illness of a key leader can all influence the impact of a congregation. So, even though this book offers biblical and practical principles that can have direct impact on the effectiveness of your church, *it is not a formula for guaranteed results.*

Still, I hope you see that *dirt matters.* The soil or culture of a church directly affects its outcomes, and one of the best ways to shape and enhance church culture is by instilling unified, healthy values into its life. These values can and should vary from congregation to congregation, but there are some values, such as the *Activators,* that are catalytic and virtually essential for a healthy culture to evolve.

Cultivating values into an existing church is hard work that takes time and intentionality. You must envision your crop by determining what God is calling your church to be and do. You need to test the soil and honestly evaluate the present state of your congregation. Then you must enter into the challenging process of breaking ground and gracefully nurturing the appropriate values into the life of the church.

In spite of all these efforts, there is no promise that the culture of your church will change. People may push back and resist the values you are advocating. Others may question your heart, your motives, and your competency. A dominant personality or a discontented family may undermine your credibility and message. Some may try to drive you out.

Yet if you are fortunate enough to see the soil quality rise, three things are guaranteed to happen. First, your church will become a healthier, Christ-centered community. There will be higher morale, more focus on the "big picture," more loyalty to Christ and the church family, a greater sense of unity, and more simplicity and speed in decision-making. There will likely be more humility, more self-sacrifice, and more spiritual growth occurring in people's lives. While still flawed, your church will be a more God-honoring community of faith.

Second, your church will be a more vibrant place. There will be more life, more passion, and more energy. Whenever God is moving and people are becoming more spiritually healthy, there is joy, zeal, and enthusiasm. You don't have to teach people to smile as if church were a Zig Ziglar seminar. Laughter and hugs will be commonplace because when the culture is healthy, the church is naturally more alive (Romans 8:11).

Finally, God will do His best work, and the ministry of your church will likely be more effective. This doesn't mean that we can dictate the outcomes. In spite of our best efforts, we must remember that Jesus is the one building His church and that God is the one who gives the growth. We cannot manipulate that growth, nor should we impose our desired results upon our sovereign Lord. Yet Jesus told us that He wants us to bear much fruit and that when the soil is good, the harvest may be thirty, sixty, or one hundred *times* what we have sown (Mark 4:20).

The fruit of your labor may not be as big as you might hope. Or it may exceed your wildest expectations. Your harvest might be visible for all to see, or it might not be manifested until after your death. Ultimately, the outcomes are God's concern. Our focus should be on staying faithful, being obedient, and making the most with what God has given us by working to improve the culture of our church.

I hope you find this encouraging as well as challenging. And I pray that God gives you the strength, courage, and wisdom to nurture and develop a better quality of soil within your church. In so doing, may you be able to see and experience what the Psalmist wrote many years ago: *"They sowed fields and planted vineyards that yielded a fruitful harvest; he blessed them, and their numbers greatly increased, and he did not let their herds diminish"* (107:37-38).

APPENDIX 1

(Examples of Church Values)

Acceptance	Accountability	Adaptability
Anticipation	Apprenticing	Authenticity
Biblical Authority	Boldness	Celebration
Character	Christlikeness	Community
Compassion	Concern for the Poor	Connection
Creativity	Dependence	Discipline
Disciple-Making	Diversity	Efficiency
Empowered Membership	Equipping Laity	Excellence
Experiencing God	Faith	Faithfulness
Family	Fellowship	Flexibility
Forgiveness	Freedom	Fun
Generosity	Gift-based Ministry	Global Emphasis
Grace	Group Life	Growth
Health	Heritage	Holiness
Honor	Humility	Humor
Incarnational Ministry	Influence	Innovation
Integrity	Journey	Joy
Justice	Kingdom Building	Life Change
Loyalty	Manifestation of the Spirit	Maturity
Miracles	Missions Focus	Morality
Movement	Multiplication	Optimism
Outward Focus	Quality	Passion
Peace	People Centered	Personal Relationship
Political Engagement	Prayer	Presence
Prophetic Voice	Reaching the Lost	Reconciliation

Relevance	Respect	Revival
Risk	Sacrifice	Sanctification
Scripture	Servant-Leadership	Service
Simplicity	Social Justice	Spirit Driven
Spiritual Direction	Stewardship of Resources	Teamwork
Testimony	Transformation	Truth
Teachable Spirit	Teaching	Unity
Urgency	Wisdom	Witnesses for Christ
Worship		

APPENDIX II

(Additional questions to ask when evaluating the culture of your church)

How old is our congregation? What are the pros and cons of this?

What are the historical attendance trends? What are the reasons for them? Do we have a glass ceiling?

What are our core stories (the ones that existing members tell over and over again)?

Do we have stories of success? What about stories of failure?

When were the good ol' days? What was happening, and why were they so good?

What is our church most proud of today? What are we most embarrassed or ashamed of?

Where does our congregation find its identity?

If Jesus were to appear and critique our ministry as He did the churches in Revelation 2-3, what might He say to us?

Does our church have unrealized dreams? Are those dreams worth holding on to, or should they be put to sleep?

Are there new dreams that might have some traction? Have we floated some trial balloons, and what kind of response have we gotten?

Does our church have a mission or vision statement? Do people know it? Do people believe it? Do the leaders own it?

Who are the influencers (the people in our church who really shape our culture and have a great deal of impact on others)? What are they like? What are the positives and potential negatives they bring to the table?

Do we have a denominational influence? How does this limit us? How does this help us? Are there resources that we can tap into?

Whom does our church attract? And who tends to stick? Are there any trends or patterns? Age? Religious background? Married, single, or families?

Do we understand the larger community around us? Have we ever looked at demographics and psycho-graphics? Would it be helpful to do so?

What external factors in our community affect our church? Are people moving here or moving out? Is there a general resistance or openness to spiritual issues?

Are there things that we can help change in our community? What are the things that we cannot control or ever change about our community?

Are there any churches in our area that are growing? If so, why? Without trying to copy them, are there things we can learn from them?

Are we willing to visit some other churches in order to see and experience what they are doing?

The Apostle Paul said, "Follow me as I follow Christ." Who are the outside people that influence our church? Other congregations? Leaders? Theologians? Writers?

What will likely never change at our church? Doctrine? Practices? Traditions?

What would absolutely flip people out? Why? Is it worth considering?

What would get the minister fired outside of moral failure and heresy?

Are we willing to invest money into a coach or consultant who will help us evaluate and chart a course?

What are the strengths and weaknesses of our facility? Location? Space? Accessibility? Aesthetics? Parking?

Does the physical look and feel of our church match the ministry we are shooting for?

Are there unique mindsets at work in our faith community?

ENDNOTES

1. Lewis touches on the subject of prioritizing second things over first things in several of his writings. In a letter to Dom Bede Griffiths on April 23, 1951, he famously wrote, "Put first things first and we get second things thrown in: put second things first and we lose both the first and the second things." The quotation about Esau comes from a 1942 essay called "First and Second Things," in which Lewis addresses the folly of people who focus on the smaller good rather than a greater good. He expresses surprise that people don't understand the only way to get and enjoy secondary blessings is to put "first things first."

2. This definition comes from an on-line article entitled "Develop Your Values and Value Statements Within Your Strategic Framework" by Susan M. Heathfield.

3. Malphurs has an entire chapter in this book dedicated to the subject of values that is very good. He also has another book entitled *Look Before You Lead*, which I highly suggest as a resource for developing values and evaluating church culture.

4. Lyle Schaller in *44 Steps Up Off the Plateau*, p. 28.

5. Steven R. Covey in *First Things First*, p. 32.

6. Samuel R. Chand says it takes a minimum of three years to change culture in *Cracking Your Church's Culture Code*, p. 103. George Barna says four years or longer in *Turnaround Churches*, p. 56. Aubrey Malphurs says two to four years in *Advanced Strategic Planning*, p. 93, but the two-year number is a quote from Ken Blanchard, who comes from a business perspective.

7. I spent one week with Dr. Larry Crabb at his School of Spiritual Direction. It was a powerful and life-changing week that I would highly suggest for anyone who feels drawn to spiritual direction and a fresh vision for spiritual formation. You can learn more at newwayministries.org.

8. Wayne Mueller in *Daily Office* by Peter Scazzero p. 108.

9. This insight comes from Warren Weirsbe and his excellent devotional book *On Being a Servant of God*.

10. Christian Schwarz in *Natural Church Development*, p 7.

11. Larry Crabb in *Real Church*, p 13.

12. Charles E. Hummel in *Tyranny of the Urgent*, p 10.

13. George Barna in *Turnaround Churches: How to Overcome Barriers to Growth and Bring New Life to an Established Church*, pp. 91, 102.

14. An example would be C. S. Lewis, who is significantly more popular among Evangelicals after his death than before. Little is said today about the non-mainstream beliefs he appeared to struggle with. Another example is Dietrich Bonhoeffer, who, though he had some amazing material on discipleship and community, was a progressive in his theology and held to some liberal views that many Evangelicals might disagree with.

15. Eugene Peterson in "Having Ears, Do You Not Hear?" in *Leadership Journal,* Winter 2009.

16. A great book that I suggest is *Accidental Pharisees* by Larry Osborne.

17. Whenever a church doubles in size, it is likely to face the Pioneer-Homesteader conflict. This conflict is based on a dynamic that occurred when people migrated West during the 19th century. When a church doubles in size, there is a practical and emotional reality that there are more "new" people than established people. This can cause longtime members to feel unsettled. When they were still in the majority, there was an unspoken sense of control and influence. Now, when they realize they are in the minority, they feel they've lost control of the church, and they begin to say things like, "This is no longer the church it once was." There is increased fear that they can no longer dictate the future direction of the congregation because the new people are driving it. When this fear hits, it's not uncommon for some sort of showdown to occur, so leaders in churches close to doubling in size should research this principle.

18. Josephus, *Against Apion, 2.8, 108.*

19. There is a book I suggest on this called *Renovation of the Church*. It is a wonderful story of a congregation's journey from an attractional model to one that focuses on spiritual formation and discipleship.

20. In *The Scandal of Father Brown.*

21. Samuel R. Chand in *Cracking Your Church's Culture Code,* p. 116.

22. As posted on Twitter

23. John Ortberg in *If You Want to Walk on Water,* p. 60

24. A few books I recommend for leadership teams are *Simple Church* by Thom Rainer, *Purpose-Driven Church* by Rick Warren, and *Church Unique* by Will Mancini. Each book has different nuances, but combined, they give a great overview and help church leaders ask the right questions. As a result, they provide great content for group discussions.

25. In Appendix II, I give some specific questions that can be used for a survey. You can contact the 95network for additional ideas as well.

26. This is a variation of a more popular business model called SWOT, which is an acrostic for Strengths, Weaknesses, Opportunities, and Threats. SWOT is primarily used to determine the feasibility of a specific project or a new product.

27. From Dave Jacobs' blog at davejacobs.net

28. By Ed Stetzer and Thom Rainer

29. At the 95network.com, we offer affordable online mentoring for pastors and church leaders. We also offer coaching opportunities and onsite consulting.

30. This was from a six-minute video entitled *Head Games* on the Leadership Network website, www.leadnet.org.

ACKNOWLEDGMENTS

First of all, I thank God. I can truly say—to God be the glory for anything worthwhile that has come out of my life and this project.

I would like to thank my wife, Stephanie, and my two boys, Timothy and Trevor. I could never have completed this without your support and encouragement. I love you and thank God for you.

To my parents, in-laws, extended relatives, and especially my uncle David, whom God used to open my eyes to the *dogma of dirt*, I say thank you.

To the elders, staff, and church family at Richwoods Christian Church—you are amazing, and I love serving God beside you.

I also want to acknowledge the people who nudged me in the process. Writing does not come easily for me, and I would just as soon not do it. But a couple of people have continually encouraged me over the years to pursue this. So, special thanks to Ann and Ed, whose encouragement, prayers, and support helped me to step out and complete this project.

I would also like to thank the numerous people who helped provide critical input on and editing suggestions for my manuscript. My assistant, Melissa, has added more value to this than words can say. I'd also like to thank Jon, Brandon, my neighbor Jennifer, Joel, Tim, Ken, Nathan, Dan, Austin, Chris, Marty, Christy, Dave, Jason, and Jay, among many others.

I would like to thank those who have been praying for me throughout this process, especially those on my prayer team, who continually lift me up on a regular basis.

To all the unspoken people who have encouraged me and spoken into my life over the years, I say thanks. If you are wondering if that includes you, the answer is likely yes.

Finally, I would like to thank: Our Redeemer Lutheran Church, Faith Assembly of God, and Denver Christian Church. The pastors and people of these churches have played a significant role in my journey, and I appreciate them more than words can say.

ABOUT THE AUTHOR

Jim Powell is the lead pastor of Richwoods Christian Church in Peoria, Illinois, and director of the 95network—a non-profit organization focused on encouraging and equipping the 95% of congregations in America that are under 800 people in size.

Through the 95network, Jim coaches, mentors, and consults with pastors and church leaders. He also speaks at conferences and seminars. To inquire about having Jim speak at your church or event, you can go to jimpowellonline. com.

After attending Columbia International University in South Carolina for one year, Jim went on to Quincy University, where he graduated with his B.A. in Theology and Religious Studies. He received his M.A. in Theology and Philosophy from Lincoln Christian Seminary.

Jim enjoys life in Peoria with his wife, Stephanie, their two boys, Timothy and Trevor, and their English Mastiff, Roxie. When he's not preaching, coaching, writing, or spending time with friends and family, he's probably watching a game—cheering on the *Fighting Illini, Kansas City Chiefs,* or the *St. Louis Cardinals.*

His published works include articles on church culture, leadership, and spiritual formation. *Dirt Matters* is his first book.